Real Twelve
Hi

Dick B.'s Reference Titles on Alcoholics Anonymous History

Paradise Research Publications, Inc., Publisher;
Good Book Publishing Company, Distributor P.O. Box 837, Kihei, HI 96753-0837
Phone/Fax: (808) 874 4876; Email: dickb@dickb.com; URL: http://www.dickb.com/index.shtml

Publisher's August 1, 2006 List of Titles by Author Dick B.

A New Way In.
A New Way Out.
Anne Smith's Journal, 1933-1939.
By the Power of God: A Guide to Early A.A. Groups & Forming Similar Groups Today.
Cured!: Proven Help for Alcoholics and Addicts.
Dr. Bob and His Library.
God and Alcoholism: Our Growing Opportunity in the 21st Century.
Good Morning!: Quiet Time, Morning Watch, Meditation, and Early A.A
Henrietta B. Seiberling: Ohio's Lady with a Cause.
Making Known The Biblical History and Roots of Alcoholics Anonymous: An Fifteen-Year Research, Writing, Publishing and Fact Dissemination Project.
New Light on Alcoholism: God, Sam Shoemaker, and A.A
The Akron Genesis of Alcoholics Anonymous.
The Books Early AAs Read for Spiritual Growth
The Conversion of Bill W.
The First Nationwide A.A. History Conference - Comments of Dick B.
The Golden Text of A.A.: God, the Pioneers, and Real Spirituality.
The Good Book and The Big Book: A.A.'s Roots in the Bible.
The Good Book-Big Book Guidebook.
The James Club: The Original A.A. Program's Absolute Essentials.
The Oxford Group & Alcoholics Anonymous.
That Amazing Grace (Clarence & Grace S.).
Turning Point: A History of Early A.A.'s Spiritual Roots and Successes.
Twelve Steps for You: Let Our Creator, A.A. History, and the Big Book Be Your Guide.
Utilizing Early A.A.'s Spiritual Roots for Recovery Today.
When Early AAs Were Cured and Why.

Why Early A.A. Succeeded: The Good Book in Alcoholics Anonymous Yesterday and Today (a Bible Study Primer)

Available through other distributors
Hope: The Story of Geraldine O. Delaney, 2d ed. (Alina Lodge)
Our Faith Community A.A. Legacy (Dick B., ed and compiler). (Came to Believe Publications)
Courage to Change (with Bill Pittman). (Hazelden)
Women Pioneers of AA (Dick B., contributor). (Hazelden)

Real Twelve Step Fellowship History

The Old School A.A. You May Not Know

Dick B.

Paradise Research Publications, Inc.
Kihei, Maui, Hawaii

Paradise Research Publications, Inc.
PO Box 837
Kihei, HI 96753-0837
(808 874 4876)
Email: dickb@dickb.com
URL: http://www.dickb.com/index.shtml

© 2006 by Anonymous
All rights reserved. Published 2006.
Printed in the United States of America

Cover Design by American Creations of Maui

This Paradise Research Publications Edition is published by arrangement with Good Book Publishing Company, PO Box 837, Kihei, HI: 96753-0837

The publication of this volume does not imply affiliation with, nor approval or endorsement from Alcoholics Anonymous World Services, Inc. The views expressed herein are solely those of the author. A.A. is a program of recovery from alcoholism–use of the Twelve Steps in connection with programs and activities which are patterned after A.A. but which address other problems, does not imply otherwise.

Note: All Bible verses quoted in this book, unless otherwise noted, are from the Authorized (or "King James") Version. The letters "KJV" are used when necessary to distinguish it from other versions.

ISBN: 1-885803-87-7

Table of Contents

1. Introduction..ix
2. Part 1: The Original A.A. Program of Recovery........................1
3. Part 2: The "Absolute Essentials" of the Good Book Program in Akron..15
4. Part 3: The Substantial Changes in A.A. from 1939 to 1955..79
5. Part 4: How Adding A History Element to Recovery Can Help the Newcomer Today..107
    Appendix...115
    Index...151

Introduction

The Purpose of Learning Twelve Step Fellowship History

Those who work in the trenches with alcoholics and addicts want to achieve something more than detoxification and a "dry drunk" with their newcomers. This, of course, starts with the idea that helping such people means something more than their abstinence and going to meetings. It can and should mean their reliance on the Creator and all the benefits of becoming one of His kids. Healing and wholeness then follow from salvation—a word derived from the Greek *sozo*.

God's Word makes clear His will as God our Saviour for all of us:

> Who will have all men to be saved, and to come unto the knowledge of the truth (1 Timothy 2:4)

Note how simple it is to see what God wants for the whole world. See John 3:16—

> For God so loved the world, that he gave his only begotten Son, that whosoever believeth in him should not perish, but have everlasting life.

Equally simple are His instructions for becoming saved, born again of His spirit, and hence one of His children. See Romans 10:9—

> That if thou shalt confess with thy mouth the Lord Jesus, and shalt believe in thine heart that God hath raised him from the dead, thou shalt be saved.

So too "coming unto the knowledge of the truth." Jesus explained in John 17:8, 17—

> For I have given them the words which thou gavest me; and they have received them, and have known surely that I came out from thee, and they have believed that thou didst send me. . . . Sanctify them through thy truth: thy word is truth.

If you want to become part of the family of God—become one of His kids—you simply confess with your mouth that Jesus is Lord and believe in your heart that God raised Him from the dead (facts the Good Book makes evident over and over). And if you want to learn the truth of which Jesus spoke, you simply study God's Word. And you'll learn about God, His son, His plan, His will, His gift to believers, His commandments, and the benefits from Him that are mentioned in part in Psalm 103.

Now what has all that got to do with the alcoholic, the addict, Twelve Step Fellowships, and recovery? In a very real sense—everything! For it was by accepting Jesus Christ as Lord and Saviour and learning about their Creator and His son from the Good Book, that early Akron AAs were cured. Yes. Cured! It was also with this foundation that alcoholics were able to develop a spiritual program of recovery in Akron, Ohio, with a documented 75% success rate, and later in Cleveland, with a 93% documented success rate. These astonishing successes should be compared to the dismal 1 to 5% rates found in today's programs.

The healings in early pioneer A.A. in Akron truly meant, for those who wanted it, salvation and everlasting life, as well as instructions for an abundant life attainable by God's children through renewing their minds and being led by the Spirit of God—the Christ in them—that God has so lovingly made possible (John 10:10, Romans 12:1-2, 8:10, 11, 14).

In other words, early AAs invented nothing new. They borrowed from the Good Book the instructions for being saved and for learning the truth about God and His will. They borrowed from medical people the idea that they were medically incurable and could not be helped by human hands. And they set out—without any Steps, without meetings, without drunkalogs, without any basic text but the Bible itself—and found newcomers who were really willing to go to any lengths to try and to learn what God could do for them that they had been unable to do for themselves.

This was a new way out from under the curse of alcoholism. Religion had plenty to offer. Medicine had very little. But the recovered alcoholics who picked up the religious and the medical tools were specially capable of being healed and specially qualified to reach other's with the message about the tools. This new way meant that they could pursue their own religious convictions with help from God, the Bible, and other believers—and do this without panning religion, church, or clergy. It also meant that they could bring the unique experience and compassion that one alcoholic has for another to carry the message and through personal, compassionate work alleviate the pain and suffering of alcoholism. They were buttressed by medical assurances that there was no help for the real alcoholic from the medical community, but that newcomers needed some medical help or hospitalization to steer them through the shoals of withdrawal. Medicine also offered them theories about why real alcoholics were unable to control their drinking.

These approaches will not be found either in most recovery fellowship groups or in most treatment programs today. The truth about them is there. But it requires locating and publicizing: It requires: (1) Early A.A.'s Christian Fellowship history. (2) Elimination of stone-throwing from the recovery camp at religion, church, God, Jesus Christ, and the Bible—an attitude all too prevalent today, and inconsistent with early A.A.'s program. (3) Elimination of stone-throwing by religion, churches, or clergy at Twelve Step programs. For this intense and flagrant opposition bewilders the Christian *in* Twelve Step groups, discourages his believing, and tends to drive him away *from and out* of A.A. to less effective or unproven groups. (4) Love, tolerance, and respect for the diversity of Twelve Step memberships, groups, and opinions; and yet also pulling no punches in supporting those who believe.

We leave this introduction with a challenge to you to learn and respect the early pioneer recovery program. The value of "old school A.A."— the A.A. of the Christian Fellowship in Akron—is that it achieved its documented 75% success rate amongst seemingly hopeless, medically incurable alcoholics who really tried, quickly followed by a documented 93% success rate amongst those in Cleveland. This compared to the failing 1 to 5% rate in today's fellowships. And we believe these figures make a strong case for learning all 12 Step History and early 12 Step history and then applying it today—whatever the fellowship, recovery program, or treatment group.

Part 1: The Original A.A. Program of Recovery

The Starting Point for Understanding

The principle that alcoholism can be cured by the power of God was accepted and applied long before the Society of Alcoholics Anonymous was founded in 1935.

The History of God's Miracles and Cures.

In Appendix Three of my book *When Early AAs Were Cured and Why*, I wrote a piece titled "Miracles Not to Be Forgotten" (pp. 143-159). As thoroughly as space permitted, I laid out the astonishing details, breadth, and number of miracles recorded in the Bible. The Bible itself qualifies as a miracle. The Old Testament is filled with miracles and healings performed by the Hand of God. No less impressive are the signs, miracles, wonders, healings, and raisings from the dead accomplished by Jesus, his apostles, and his disciples and recorded in the four Gospels and Acts. The Biblical healings come to life in the Book of Acts for those who choose to become born again of God's spirit and perform the same miracles that Jesus performed by acting in the name of Jesus Christ and employing the power of the Holy Spirit which the death and resurrection of Jesus had enabled them to receive. In the Appendix of this title, I've listed again the healing records of the New Testament. And these were not lost in the studies of early AAs. Healing accounts in *When Early AAs Were Cured* go on through apostolic times, healings by church fathers, and healings within the church for some 2000 years thereafter. My documented material also specifies the healings by the power of God that have been accomplished from 1800 to date, many of which were actually recorded and specified in books on healing that A.A. co-founder Dr. Bob studied and circulated among early AAs and their families.

The Cures in Early A.A.

What about alcoholism? Was God somehow uniquely limited in His power to help, heal, and cure alcoholics and addicts? Certainly not in the view of the earliest AAs. The first three AAs—Bill Wilson, Dr. Bob Smith, and Bill Dotson—all specifically stated that the "Lord" had cured them of alcoholism. Their claims generated hundreds of statements over the next ten years by AAs all over the United States who were reported by newspapers and magazines to have been cured of their malady.

In fact, it was not until a lay therapist named Richard Peabody (who actually died drunk) wrote a book titled *The Common Sense of Drinking* that the "no cure" nix was laid on the alcoholic. Out of the blue, Bill Wilson adopted for his 1939 basic text two basic ideas from Peabody's book that were to change A.A. and feed the treatment industry for decades to come. The two expressions were "There is no cure for alcoholism" and "Once an alcoholic always an alcoholic." And this negative, faithless duo of ideas caused AAs to scurry about changing literature, changing descriptions, and attempting to change or at least bury the early history of healings and replace it with a "daily reprieve" tied to a recovery that ultimately was defined as a "personality change." See *Alcoholics Anonymous*, 4th ed., Appendix II.

Why bring up this accomplished, and complete obliteration of A.A. cures today? The reasons are several: (1) The statements are false. (2) They fly in the face of a decade of statements within A.A. ranks that cures had been accomplished and were available to those who were willing to trust in God. (3) They seem to have derived from several bizarre ideas that came neither from A.A. sources, nor from medicine, nor from religion, nor even from scientific studies of earlier years. Note the steps downward from God to meetings: (a) The first bizarre piece of writing was penned by Bill Wilson during a period of severe depression, in which Bill contended that you could make the A.A. group your "higher power" if you wished. (b) This "higher power" idea cannot be found in the Bible, but it is the darling of those who have chosen to broaden A.A.'s "deity" to mean a radiator, a light bulb, the Big Dipper, Ralph, a Coke bottle, a chair, and a host of other nonsensical and idolatrous figures and figurines. Today, some of

A.A.'s paid staff frequently write and publish statements that you can believe your higher power is "Something" or "Somebody" or nothing at all. And this nonsense leaves one hard-pressed to defend the role of the Creator in A.A. at all. (c) This new and self-made recovery religion, and absurd names for *a* god, were further amplified when a former alcoholic priest turned scholar wrote a dissertation titled "Not-God" and contended, and contends to this day, that A.A. is really about "not-god-ness." Though the concept finds no support in A.A. history, the writer has become the darling of academia and is frequently quoted by those involved in grant research, technical articles, and scientific studies. Even drunks often talk more about the idea that you are not God, than the idea that God is God—the only true living Creator. This idolatry has seldom been challenged by AAs due to ignorance of their own history. Nor by many religious writers who either reject A.A. as heretical or idolatrous or simply do not know its early history, Biblical roots, and original Christian fellowship. Christian writers sometimes simply fluff off A.A.'s recovery religion as convoluted but "practical"—buying into the ambiguous dogma, "**It** works."

The Turn-about Required for Believers.

If an individual AA such as myself, or a group of AAs, or a group of 12 Step activists, or a Christian recovery or treatment group, or clergy, or inquiring scholars and physicians are to find God in A.A. at all today, they are going to have to concede what A.A. pioneers clearly acknowledge: God is not dead. He is the one, true, living Creator. He is the power to whom A.A. pioneers turned for cure, and it is He who made available the power that cured them.

It should be clear from this title that the preponderance of evidence defining the nature, principles, practices, and value of A.A. lies with its original thesis: A.A. has no monopoly on God, but it is founded on the principle that a cure can be attained through conversion and the establishment of a relationship with the "One who has all power"—"God," as AAs specifically described Him in the very beginning language introducing their suggested Twelve Steps of Recovery. What was that? "The One with all power. That one is God. May you find Him now!"

In fact, if one delves into recovery history far enough, he or she should become convinced that the Godly principles in the early A.A. Christian Fellowship were those which had been taken primarily from the Bible and used for many centuries to help alcoholics get well—eras long before A.A. was founded.

The Akron A.A. Christian Program That Cured Alcoholics

Beginning with 1934, A.A. Co-founder Bill Wilson said many times that he was unable to get a single person sober in the six months that he scurried from Towns Hospital to Calvary Rescue Mission to Oxford Group meetings in New York. Bill feverishly chased drunks, but not one of them got sober. Furthermore, as Bill began bringing drunks to the home that he and Lois Wilson shared, the result was the same for several years. Not one person got sober. And even in the earliest years of New York A.A., the best Wilson could claim was that his partner Hank Parkhurst got sober—only to drink at a later point; and that John Henry Fitzhugh Mayo—son of an Episcopal minister—was the other newcomer who was reached successfully by Bill.

Let's therefore begin with, and focus on, the Akron program of 1935 to 1938, that Bill and Co-founder Dr. Bob developed *together*. It was the successful one. It was the program that, by 1937, had produced forty alcoholic recoveries among men with two years or less of continuous sobriety. Counting noses at that time, Bill and Bob found they had a total success record of 50% among these men, with a further, additional 25% success record among pioneers who relapsed but returned to sobriety. That's where the 75% success rate among AAs who really tried became traceable.

The Frank Amos Written Summary of the Pioneer Program

The Early AAs' solution to their problems was reliance on the Creator. That reliance produced the astonishing success rates among the medically incurable alcoholics who really tried. It's a story worth learning. It is simple. The approach was effective. Note also that, because it worked, it attracted thousands to A.A. over the ensuing years. Medical cures and percentages of cure are what attract patients. Medical failures do not. Fortunately, we still have a precise and accurate study of the Akron program that succeeded. Details that you can use this very day.

After A.A. was founded, Bill Wilson had come to John D. Rockefeller, Jr., looking for money. Bill told the famous businessman the results Dr. Bob and his helpers were achieving in Akron. And Rockefeller decided to see for himself. He sent his agent Frank Amos out to Akron to investigate, and Amos reported back in two different papers exactly what he found. Amos had spent about a week in Akron, interviewed Dr. Bob and members of his fellowship, interviewed their wives, interviewed an Akron judge, an Akron attorney, medical colleagues, and others. And the following is the essence of the program, as Amos described it to Rockefeller:

- An alcoholic must realize that he is an alcoholic, incurable from a medical viewpoint, and that he must never drink anything with alcohol in it.
- He must surrender himself absolutely to God, realizing that in himself there is no hope.
- Not only must he want to stop drinking permanently, he must remove from his life other sins such as hatred, adultery, and others which frequently accompany alcoholism. Unless he will do this absolutely, Smith and his associates refuse to work with him.
- He must have devotions every morning–a "quiet time" of prayer and some reading from the Bible and other religious literature. Unless this is faithfully followed, there is grave danger of backsliding.
- He must be willing to help other alcoholics get straightened out. This throws up a protective barrier and strengthens his own willpower and convictions.
- It is important, but not vital, that he meet frequently with other reformed alcoholics and form both a social and a religious comradeship.
- Important, but not vital, that he attend some religious service at least once weekly.

Seven points, the last two—religious comradeship and church attendance—were simply *recommended*, but not required. The foregoing original A.A. program in Akron had no steps—twelve, six, or otherwise. It had no basic text but the Bible. For reading matter, it did circulate among the early fellowship members a large number of Christian books, devotionals, and articles. And you can read for yourself the foregoing detailed description of their program in *DR. BOB and the Good Oldtimers*. NY: Alcoholics Anonymous World Services, Inc., 1980, pp. 130-136. You can find their reading materials in Dick B. *The Books Early AAs Read for Spiritual Growth*, 7th ed.

But the Frank Amos reports merely summarized the requirements of the program. Amos did not describe its activities with any particularity, and they need to be examined more fully. Though accurate as Amos set the requirement points forth, the importance of the original requirements and practices is not clear without a description of several additional details Amos didn't cover. Therefore, we've reconstructed from historical research a picture of the entire spiritual program of recovery developed in Akron between 1935 and 1938, clearly comprehending the details summarized by Frank Amos.

The Specifics of What the Pioneers Did in Akron

They located and "qualified" a "real" alcoholic who needed help, wanted help, and would do whatever was expected of him: In the case of the first three AAs—Bill Wilson, Dr. Bob Smith, and Bill Dotson—someone had actually gone searching for each of the three men as "pigeons" needing help. Later, wives and relatives would sometimes bring a new man to Dr. Bob for help. Sometimes drunks appeared on the scene and asked for help. But searching out and "qualifying" the new person as one who was serious and willing was a critical part of the new program. He was interrogated to verify these points. And that very outreach itself contributed mightily to the success of the newcomer and of his benefactors. All learned that you can't make a drunk quit unless he wants to, but you can provide him with a personal testimony of success that has clout

They usually hospitalized the newcomer for about seven days: Hospitalization and/or medical help for a brief period was virtually a "must" for almost all the early A.A. members. Then, as now, there was danger of seizures, severe shaking, injury to self, and disorientation.

Medical monitoring was considered prudent. During that period, only a Bible was allowed in the hospital room. Medications were administered. There were daily visits and lengthy talks by Dr. Bob with each patient. There were regular visits by recovered pioneers who apprised the newcomer of their own stories and successes. Just prior to discharge, there was a visit to the newcomer by Dr. Bob. He may have covered additional points about alcoholism, such as they were known at that time. But, primarily, he asked the new person to acknowledge his belief in the Creator. If there was an affirmative answer, Dr. Bob required the patient to make a "surrender" to Christ on his knees and join Dr. Bob in a prayer. And release from the hospital followed.

They often offered food, shelter, and support in the home of some pioneer family. The two homes that first come to mind are those of Dr. Bob and his wife Anne Smith, and Wally G. and his wife Annabelle. In a sense, these live-in arrangements represented the first "half-way" houses as they are often called today. Recovery work in Akron did not begin or take place in groups or meetings or treatment centers; nor in rehabs or therapy or confinement. It took place primarily in homes, and that, in itself, constituted a very different situation from any program or practice of the Oxford Group where Bill Wilson had previously cut his teeth in the New York area. The men in Akron were fed, sheltered, and given a long-term healing opportunity.

As stated, Akron pioneer efforts took place primarily in the homes of people like Dr. Bob and Anne Smith. And in these homes, there were: (1) Daily get-togethers. (2) Bible studies and the reading of Christian literature and devotionals circulated by Dr. Bob and his wife. (3) Quiet times held by each of the individuals who then prayed, studied the Bible, and sought God's guidance on their own. (4) Morning quiet time meetings led by Dr. Bob's wife for AAs and their families who listened to Anne teach from the Bible, prayed together, heard Anne share from her spiritual journal, discussed its contents with those present, and then sought guidance from God for the day. (5) Residents frequently discussed problems and Biblical solutions with Dr. Bob, Henrietta Seiberling, T. Henry Williams, and Anne Smith. Bob was inclined to ask: "What does the Good Book say?" Also, the old Christian Endeavor question: "What would Jesus do?" And those who stayed over many days and nights, in this or that home, broke bread, lived, and fellowshipped together. (6) Once a week the pioneers held a "regular" Wednesday meeting with "real" surrenders upstairs after the manner of James 5:15-16. (7) Pioneers utilized a few of some twenty-eight Oxford Group life-changing practices such as Inventory,

Confession, Conviction, and Restitution. (8) They then arranged visits to newcomers at the hospital. (9) They recommended church attendance by most. (10) They enjoyed social, religious, and family fellowship. (11) And it all began again.

There was one "Regular" weekly meeting on Wednesdays at the home of T. Henry and Clarace Williams in Akron. Though it originally began as an Oxford Group meeting, it was not conducted like most Oxford Group meetings. Its members—Oxford Group members, alcoholics, wives and children—were there to help alcoholics get well by spiritual means. Host T. Henry therefore called the meeting a "clandestine lodge" of the Oxford Group because it differed so much from the movement Frank Buchman and Sam Shoemaker were leading and in which a few East Coast AAs like Bill Wilson had participated. Also, before the Wednesday meeting, leaders such as Dr. Bob, Anne, Henrietta Seiberling, and Mr. and Mrs. Williams would hold a Monday "setup" meeting where God's guidance was sought as to who should lead the Wednesday meeting and what its topic should be. On Wednesdays, there were none of the conventional Oxford Group testimonials nor were there any of what have today become alcoholic drunkalogs. The regular meeting opened with a prayer. Scripture was read, then group prayer, and then a brief group guidance circle. The meeting discussed a selected topic—whether from the Bible, a devotional, or a subject involving living by Biblical principles. The discussion was led by someone such as Dr. Bob, Henrietta Seiberling, or T. Henry Williams. There was intense focus on the study and discussion of the Bible's Book of James, Sermon on the Mount, and 1 Corinthians 13. There was a special time for "real" surrenders upstairs for the newcomers. Following those, arrangements were made downstairs for some in the group to visit newcomers at the Akron City Hospital. The meeting closed with the Lord's Prayer; socializing; and the exchange of Christian literature displayed on tables for the taking. There had been no drunkalogs. No Steps. No Big Book. No texts at all. Just the Bible and devotionals like *The Upper Room* and the specially valued lessons taught from James, Corinthians, and Matthew. One naïve historian has referred to all this as bibliotherapy—apparently trying to convey the thought that the pioneers were trying to heal and change by "reading." The same historian saw A.A. as the epitome of "not-god-ness." But the most basic study of early A.A. history makes it clear that the Akronites were working for a relationship with the Creator, learning how to fellowship with the Creator and His son, learning His expectations as to obedience—abhorring evil and cleaving that that which was good. In other words, if one became a child of God, behaved as a child of God, and diligently sought God, God Himself rewarded those who sought Him. See Hebrews 11:6.

"Real Surrenders" to Christ, several Oxford Group practices, counseling with the Smiths and Henrietta Seiberling, study of Christian literature, and church attendance.

(1) Real surrenders: In order to belong to the Akron fellowship, newcomers had to make a "real surrender." This was akin to the altar call at rescue missions or the confession of Christ with other believers in churches, except that it was a very small, private, ceremony which took place upstairs and away from the regular meeting. Four A.A. old-timers (Ed Andy from Lorain, Ohio; J. D. Holmes from Indiana; Clarence Snyder from Cleveland; and Larry Bauer in Akron) have all independently verified orally and in writing that the Akron surrenders required acceptance of Jesus Christ as Lord and Saviour. Those conversions took place at the regular Wednesday meeting upstairs in the manner described in James 5:15-16. Kneeling, with "elders" at his side, the newcomer accepted Christ and, with the prayer partners, asked God to take alcohol out of his life and to help, guide, and strengthen him to live by cardinal Christian teachings such as those in the Oxford Group's Four Absolutes—Honesty, Purity, Unselfishness, and Love.

(2) Life-changing practices from the Oxford Group: Not so clear as to Akron is just how many of its pioneers completed such Oxford Group life-changing practices as Inventory, Confession, Conviction, and Restitution though there is certainly mention of some.

(3) Counseling, Bible Study, Life problems, Family issues: Many men and women received counseling from Bob and Anne Smith, Henrietta Seiberling, and T. Henry Williams. They frequently studied or listened to Scripture, prayed, and discussed practical Christian living principles involved in their jobs and family difficulties. Anne Smith worked extensively with new people and their families and formed a Woman's Group in Akron in A.A.'s second year—long before Al-Anon came into being..

(4) Widespread reading of Christian literature: Dr. Bob, His wife Anne, Henrietta Seiberling, and others fed AAs and their families a wide variety of literature on the Bible, prayer, healing, love, the life of Christ, Shoemaker's writings, Oxford Group books, and daily study

topics. These were circulated around the fellowship and read by alcoholics and family members alike.

(5) The Church Option: Though present-day A.A. literature is devoid of significant mention of church, the Amos reports disclose that attendance at a church of one's choice was recommended. There is particular evidence that Roman Catholics were in touch with their own priests from the beginning, and that the leaders—Bob, Anne, Henrietta, and Mr. and Mrs. Williams—all attended churches in Akron.

Quiet Times: (held by individuals, by the group, and by the early birds in the morning with Anne Smith). The first condition of receiving revelation is *not* "listening" to God. The first condition of effective communication with the Creator is the establishing of one's standing as a child of God by accepting Jesus Christ as Lord and Saviour. With that accomplished, the new Christian is a member of the body of Christ, able to communicate with God and His son, and endowed with the ability to understand spiritual matters the "natural man" cannot comprehend. Hence, this was a vital part of the Akron program–evidenced by the "surrender" at the hospital and certainly the "real surrender" in the homes. Then, for these born-again believers, quiet time consisted of reading the Bible; prayer to and seeking revelation from, God; studying devotionals like *The Upper Room* and *The Runner's Bible*; utilizing *Anne Smith's Journal* for teaching and instruction; and reading Christian literature such as Henry Drummond's *The Greatest Thing in the World,* Nora Smith Holm's *The Runner's Bible, The Upper Room,* and various studies of the Sermon on the Mount by Oswald Chambers, Glenn Clark, Harry Emerson Fosdick, Emmet Fox, and E. Stanley Jones.

Intensive personal work with newcomers: Dr. Bob was called the "Prince of Twelfth Steppers" and worked personally with over 5000 alcoholics aiming at their recovery and cure. Visits with newcomers by those who had already made the grade were a regular occurrence in Akron. And, though Bill's personal outreach efforts yielded little fruit in the East, when compared to the results in Akron, Bill Wilson was the original, vigorous hustler—seeking out new people at Oxford Group meetings, Towns Hospital, and Calvary Rescue Mission. Topping even that personal work, however, was the unquestioned, liveliest individual 12 Stepping by young Clarence H. Snyder. Before he formed the Cleveland group, Clarence was bringing alcoholics down to Akron on a regular basis. In Cleveland, Clarence was a dynamo seeking out drunks, taking them through Step classes, and getting new groups going. Cleveland groups grew from one to thirty in a year. And Clarence sponsored hundreds through the years—finally as the AA with the longest period of sobriety.

Self-government, self-leadership, and self-support within membership groups: Both Dr. Bob and Bill were raised in the tradition of the New England Congregational denominations. This meant that each Congregational church was governed by its members. It was supported by its members. And it was accountable to no higher person, power, official, office, or administration than the rule and vote of its own congregation. Whatever the way by which this concept reached A.A., this system became the rule for local A.A. groups though Dr. Bob was undeniably the "leader" in Akron in the early pioneer days. At the same time, Bob was always opposed to transferring control of the A.A. fellowship to New York or some central administration there.

Helping wives and families. The earliest AAs were male. Yet the earliest A. A. meetings in Akron were family affairs. Alkies, their wives, and their children would attend the meetings at the home of T. Henry and Clarence Williams. Oxford Group activists in Akron participated in the same way. Henrietta Seiberling made sure all her children attended some of the meetings. The Smith kids attended many. Wives of members worked shoulder-to-shoulder with their husbands. The names of these women are laid out in *DR. BOB and the Good Oldtimers.* Thus the work of T. Henry had the help of his wife Clarace. The work of Dr. Bob, that of Anne. The work of Wally G., that of his wife Annabelle. The work of Tom Lucas, that of his wife. And the work of Clarence Snyder, that of his wife Dorothy. But there were special needs of wives of alcoholics that began to be recognized right away. Anne Smith was at the head of the pack in meeting them. Throughout early A.A. personal stories, you find remarks that Anne was legendary with newcomers, that she was especially kind to wives, that as early as 1936, she formed a women's group, and that she was particularly helpful to Lois Wilson time and time again. Her crown jewel, of course, is *Anne Smith's Journal, 1933-1939*, which she wrote and used for teaching during all of A.A.'s formative years. Anne's journal is filled with materials as suitable for dealing with the problems of family as with the alcoholic himself. Yet it's rarely mentioned even by A.A. historians, and never in A.A. literature itself. It's not my purpose to deal with women's issues or rights, or the absence of women as members of the earliest A.A. But it is quite clear that Anne Smith, Bob, Bill to some extent, and Lois later realized that the special problems of what some now call "the family disease" of alcoholism needed to be addressed, both for the sake of individuals, of those who suffer, and for A.A. itself. Even Lois Wilson huddled in New York with her little "kitchen group" for quite some time before the seeds of Al-Anon and its Family Groups began to appear and take root. She openly sought and appreciated the help of Anne Smith.

The Emphasis of Bob and Bill together: I have several times quoted or summarized the statements of Bob and Bill together on the platform of the Shrine Auditorium in Los Angeles in 1943. Their remarks were reported in the March, 1943 issue of *The Tidings*. About 4500 AAs and their families were present. Bill spoke about the importance of Divine Aid, the religious element in A.A., and prayer. Dr. Bob spoke about the importance of cultivating the habit of prayer and reading the Bible. Both men were warmly received–a testimony to their harmonious accord, consistency, and simplicity of presentation when appearing together. The event signaled the unanimity of intent, if not of experience and knowledge, between Bill and Bob.

The Two Distinctly Different A.A. Roots, Ideas, and Programs

Present day histories, writings, and AAs have become so accustomed to an erroneous A.A. history timeline that it is often difficult for them to see the difference between the Akron program and the New York program and to understand why believers need to hear and learn the Akron program first. The following book arrived in my mail only this morning and shows how corrupted historical knowledge has persuaded serious workers of a totally new and different A.A. Classifying A.A. in a chapter on "Support People," the authors wrote:

> The most well-known support group is Alcoholics Anonymous (AA), founded in the 1930s by people who had tried many other methods of abstaining from alcohol and failed. They found that mutual support gave them a tool that enabled them to do what had previously been unattainable. . . . Alcoholics Anonymous is especially helpful for individuals who prefer a spiritually-based group. The steps of AA are spiritual in nature. In AA you are encouraged to accept the help of a higher power, though that power can be defined as you choose. It can even be

the power of the group itself. Merline Miller and David Miller. *Staying Clean & Sober: Complementary and Natural Srategies for Healing the Addicted* Brain. Orem, Utah, Woodland Publishing, 2005, p. 171.

The Miller language classifies AAs and A.A. as "support people," a "spiritually-based group," seeking "help of a higher power," believing "that power can be defined as you choose," and instructing people that this higher power can be "the power of the group itself." I'm not singling out these authors. I could list dozens of contemporary writings to the same effect. See Dick B., *God and Alcoholism.* In fact, you can pick up just about any piece of A.A. Conference Approved literature and see the same A.A. recovery religion language. And—though it represents a total reconstruction by professionals and unbelievers—it certainly is not the A.A. that was fashioned by Bill and Dr. Bob in Akron and authorized to be described in a basic text.

I have written about that program in *The Akron Genesis of Alcoholics Anonymous.* I have also recently written about its roots and uniquely different recovery ideas.

In brief, the Akron program derived from the Christian training Dr. Bob had as a youth in St. Johnsbury, Vermont. For it was there that he and his family regularly attended the North Congregational Church four or five times a week, and that he became a member in the Church's Christian Endeavor Society. That Christian Endeavor group followed a program strikingly similar to the one Dr. Bob formulated and led in Akron many years later. Christian Endeavor involved: (1) Confession of Christ. (2) Bible Study Meetings. (3) Prayer meetings. (3) Conversion meetings. (4) Reading of religious literature with topical discussions. (5) Quiet Hour. (6) The slogans—love and service—later to become Dr. Bob's description of the essence of the A.A. program itself. These very same items comprised the heart of the Akron program.

The New York program—much more familiar to today's recovery people—had entirely different origins, influences, and practices. It also, in the years of Bill's depression began to be spun off in new and surprising directions. And these will be discussed later in this history.

Part 2: The "Absolute Essentials" of the Good Book Program in Akron

Undoubtedly, the most ignored, deleted, and omitted part of A.A. history is not only that pertaining to the Bible itself, but also to the three parts thereof which Dr. Bob said were absolutely essential to the early program. Those parts were not viewed as "bibliotherapy." They involved the Word of God, the will of God, obedience to God, the love of God, and prayer to God, to mention just a few items. These parts were mentioned specifically by Bob and Bill, but not in A.A.'s Big Book. These parts were actually read regularly in the early meetings. And the ideas from the three segments not only formed the basis for early A.A. principles, practices, and cures, but also for basic ideas in the Big Book and Twelve Step ideas Bill wrote in his Big Book published in 1939.

Comments by Bill W. and Dr. Bob about James, the Sermon on the Mount, 1 Corinthians 13

Dr. Bob pointed out that there were no twelve steps at the beginning, that "our stories didn't amount to anything to speak of," and that they [A.A.'s "older ones"] were "convinced that the answer to their problems was in the Good Book" *DR. BOB*, p. 96).

A.A. Old-timer Clarence Snyder pointed out as to Dr. Bob: "If someone asked him a question about the program, his usual response was: 'What does it say in the Good Book?'" *DR. BOB*, p. 144. Bob said quite clearly: "I didn't write the Twelve Steps. I had nothing to do with the writing of them" but that "We already had the basic ideas, though not in terse and tangible form. We got them as a result of our study of the Good Book" *DR. BOB*, pp. 96-97. Dr. Bob stressed over and over that the "the parts we found absolutely essential were" the Book of James, the Sermon on the Mount, and 1 Corinthians 13 *(e.g. DR. BOB*, p. 96). In the Foreword Dr. Bob's son "Smitty" wrote for my book, *The Good Book and The Big Book*, "Smitty" pointed to the importance in A.A. of James, the Sermon, and Corinthians; and I heard

15

Smitty repeat his statement at several large A.A. history meetings, including one at A.A.'s San Diego International Convention in 1995. Dr. Bob's sponsee Clarence Snyder, got sober in February of 1938 and later became the AA with the greatest amount of sobriety. Clarence often echoed Dr. Bob's words about the Bible and the three essential parts. Also, in a talk given to AAs in Glenarden, Maryland, on August 8, 1981, Clarence said: "This program emanates from the Sermon on the Mount and the Book of James. If you want to know where this program came from, read the fifth, sixth, seventh chapters of Matthew. Study it over and over, and you'll see the whole program in there" Glen Cove, NY: Glenn K. Audio Tape #2451.

Bill Wilson had gotten sober in New York at Towns Hospital in late 1934. He went to Akron on a business deal, and met Dr. Bob Smith at Henrietta Seiberling's Gate House. Shortly thereafter, at Anne Smith's suggestion, Bill moved in with the Smiths. Though not particularly accurate in its characterization of the daily Bible readings at the Smith home, one official A.A. history says:

> Bill now joined Bob and Anne in the Oxford Group practice of having morning guidance sessions together, with Anne reading from the Bible [Note: Oxford Group 'guidance' did often involve reading from the Bible, but the Smith-Wilson Bible studies were inappropriately called 'guidance sessions'; the studies were directed at the Bible itself, at prayer, at literature, and at such revelation from their Heavenly Father as they chose to seek]

> [The A.A. account continues:]. Reading. . . from her chair in the corner, she would softly conclude, 'Faith without works is dead.' "As Dr. Bob described it, they were 'convinced that the answer to our problems was in the Good Book. To some of us older ones, the parts that we found absolutely essential were the Sermon on the Mount [Matthew, Chapters 5-7], the 13th chapter of First Corinthians, and the Book of James. **The Book of James was considered so important, in fact, that some early members even suggested The James Club as a name for the Fellowship'.**" See *Pass It On*. NY: Alcoholics Anonymous World Services, Inc., 1984, p. 147; emphasis added.

Published four years earlier, and written by a different author, another A.A. "Conference Approved" history tells the facts somewhat more accurately. Thus *DR. BOB and the Good Oldtimers* NY: Alcoholics Anonymous World Services, Inc., 1980, states at p. 71:

> "For the next three months [after Bill met Bob in May of 1935], I [Bill] lived with these two wonderful people," Bill said. "I shall always believe they gave me more than I ever brought them." Each morning, there was a devotion, he recalled. After a long silence, in which they awaited inspiration and guidance, Anne would read from the Bible. "James was our favorite," he said. "Reading from her chair in the corner, she would softly conclude, 'Faith without works is dead.' This was a favorite quotation of Anne's, much as **the Book of James was a favorite with early A.A.'s—so much so that 'The James Club' was favored by some as a name for the Fellowship'"** (emphasis added).

In his own history of early A.A., Bill Wilson wrote:

> And we could remember Anne as she sat in the corner by the fireplace, reading from the Bible the warning of James, that "faith without works is dead." *Alcoholics Comes of Age*. NY: Alcoholics Anonymous World Services, Inc., 1967, p. 7.

John R. was a well-known, long-lived Akron A.A. old-timer. And John specifically recalled as to these matters that much of the work on the writing of the Big Book "went on the Q.T." He said the average member wasn't aware of it. Then, as to the name Alcoholics Anonymous that was proposed for the Big Book, John R. tells us this in *DR. BOB*, p. 213:

> "Take the name A.A., for instance," said John. "The people here in Akron didn't like it, and they were saying no. Wally G.—said, **'Hey, what's with this A.A. deal? We want to call it Saint James.'** But Doc knew all the time that they were going to call it A.A. . . . They had it that way before we knew it. Then it dawned on Wally that he was arguing against

it and they had already named it. Boy, that used to make him sore! But he was a guy" (emphasis added).

Historian Bill Pittman wrote of an alleged "**Dr. Bob's Required Reading List**"—among his five named "required" items. Pittman placed first on his list "The Holy Bible, King James Version. The Sermon on the Mount, the Lord's Prayer, The Book of James, The 13th Chapter of First Corinthians" Bill Pittman, *AA The Way It Began*. Seattle: Glen Abbey Books, 1988, p. 197; emphasis added.

In his last major address to AAs in 1948, **Dr. Bob said:**

> When we started in on Bill D. [A.A. Number Three], we had no Twelve Steps. . . . But we were convinced that the **answer to our problems** was in the Good Book. To some of us older ones, the parts that we found **absolutely essential were** the Sermon on the Mount, the thirteenth chapter of First Corinthians, and the Book of James. . . . *The Co-Founders of Alcoholics Anonymous. Biographical sketches their last major talks*. NY: Alcoholics Anonymous World Services, Inc., 1972, 1975, pp. 9-10, emphasis added.

In a pamphlet published by the Friday Forum Luncheon Club of the Akron A.A. Groups, the pamphlet's writer selected the following from a "lead" [talk] given by Dr. Bob in Youngstown, Ohio:

> Members of Alcoholics Anonymous begin the day with a prayer for strength and a short period of Bible reading. **They find the basic messages they need in** the Sermon on the Mount, in Corinthians **and the Book of James.** Dick B., *The Good Book and The Big Book: A.A's Roots in the Bible,* 2d ed, Kihei, HI: Paradise Research Publications, Inc., 1997, p 21; emphasis added.

A pamphlet published by "AA of Akron," and written at the request of Dr. Bob states:

> **There is the Bible that you haven't opened for years. Get acquainted with it. Read it with an open mind.** You will

find things that will amaze you. You will be convinced that certain passages were written with you in mind. Read the Sermon on the Mount (Matthew V, VI, and VII). Read St. Paul's inspired essay on love (I Corinthians XIII). Read the Book of James. Read the Twenty-third and Ninety-first Psalms. **These readings are brief but so important.** Dick B., *The Good Book and The Big Book, supra*, p. 20; emphasis added.

As we will discuss shortly, Nora Smith Holm's *The Runner's Bible: Spiritual Guidance for People on The Run.* Colorado: Acropolis Books, Publisher, 1998 Edition was very popular in pioneer A.A. and used particularly by Dr. Bob .That devotional was filled with references to verses in James that became part and parcel of A.A. language and ideas. See pp.16, 46, 51, 73, 79, 81, 86-87, 95-98, 100-101, 106, 110, 121, 126-127, 139, 152, 181, 184, 186, 221, 230, 245-246. And I found virtually the same plethora of relevant James quotations in the four years of quarterlies published *by The Upper Room* between 1935 and 1939, which materials were in daily use by the pioneers. Bill Wilson's secretary Nell Wing has also written a good bit on the Bible study and emphasis in early A.A.

Our Study of Book of James

Identifiable Spillovers in A.A.'s Big Book and 12 Steps from the Book of James

To avoid repeating materials in the next two sections, I'll state first that there are many quotes, references, and ideas in the Book of James that regularly appeared in early A.A. writing and practices. The following are a few:

"Faith without works is dead" was practically the parental verse among the ideas that bounced around early A.A. from James. The verse itself is quoted or paraphrased several times in the Big Book. The verse was allegedly the favorite Bible verse of Anne Smith, Dr. Bob's wife (though that theory has not been documented).The verse was allegedly Bill Wilson's favorite, along with the Book of James. And expressions said to have come from this verse were and are common in A.A. Thus Wilson named his Big Book promotional and publishing corporation

"Works Publishing Company." The shortest sentence in A.A.'s Big Book is "It works." Big Book Chapter Five is titled "How it Works;" and the first part of that chapter is read at the beginning of many A.A. meetings. Most every A.A. meeting ends with the formation of a circle in which the members join hands, join in reciting either the Lord's Prayer or the Serenity Prayer, and by shaking their arms up and down and shouting, "Keep coming back. It Works." See also Kurtz, *Not-God*, pp. 68-69; Raphael, *Bill W. and Mr. Wilson*, pp. 116-17.

"Confess your faults one to another"—though modified and amplified by the Oxford Group, by Rev. Sam Shoemaker, and by Bill's Fifth Step and its discussion language—James 5:16 has been almost universally acknowledged to be the basic source idea from James 5:16 for Step Five.

"But the tongue can no man tame: it is an unruly evil full of deadly poison"—In his last talk to AAs, Dr. Bob cautioned the fellowship to "guard that erring member the tongue." And Anne Smith made similar comments in the spiritual journal she kept and shared with early AAs and their families.

"Thou shalt love thy neighbor as thyself"—Of course, this sentence can be found in many Bible passages in addition to the one in James. It is called "The royal law according to the scripture" in James 2:8. And the verse is paraphrased in the Big Book.

"Father of lights"—**a reference** to Almighty God in James 1:17. Bill quoted this phrase, but misspelled it in his Big Book. He often mentioned it in talks to A.A. members. He spoke of the "Father of lights" who presides over us all.

The words and phrases in the following sections will illustrate how many other basic A.A. ideas came from the Book of James, though they were not actually quotes of chapter and verse and did not provide appropriate attribution.

Specific Pioneer A.A. Ideas from James

Again, to avoid undue repetition of the detailed study in the following James section, we will merely highlight here some of the key James ideas that seem to resemble words and phrases AAs adopted.

Patience.

Avoiding temptation.

Asking wisdom of God with unwavering faith.

Enduring temptation.

Recognizing that resisting temptation is man's responsibility, not God's.

Laying aside wrath and filthiness and receiving the Word of God with meekness.

Being a "doer of the word," not a hearer only.

Purporting to be religious, yet failing to bridle the tongue.

Confirming that "pure" and "undefiled religion" includes visiting the fatherless and widows and keeping yourself unspotted from the world.

Not being a respecter of persons in well-doing.

Fulfilling the royal law to love thy neighbor as thyself.

Keeping all God's commandments, not just the ones you like.

Accompanying faith with works.

Taming the tongue.

Recognizing that envying and strife are the product of "devilish" "wisdom."

Realizing that wisdom from above is pure, peaceable, gentle, full of mercy and good fruits, and without partiality or hypocrisy.

Realizing that asking amiss in prayer comes from asking to consume the object of your prayer upon your own lusts.

Knowing God resists the proud, but gives grace to the humble.

Submitting yourselves to God. Resisting the devil, and believing he will flee from you.

Drawing near to God knowing He will draw near to you.

Humbling yourselves in the sight of the Lord, and knowing He shall lift you up.

Avoiding speaking evil of, or judging, other brethren.

Saying that if the Lord will, you will live, and do this or that.

Knowing you are to do works that God's defines as good, and that doing what is not good—as that is defined in the Bible—is sin.

Holding no grudges.

Eschewing swearing.

If you are sick, summoning the elders of the church and letting them pray over you.

Believing this prayer of faith shall save the sick, and the Lord shall raise you up and forgive your sins.

Confessing your faults one to another

Praying for one another that you may be healed.

Believing that the effectual fervent prayer of a righteous man avails much.

Knowing that he who converts a sinner from the error of his way shall save a soul from death, and shall hide a multitude of sins.

You can find these principles in the writings of Rev. Sam Shoemaker, in various issues of *The Upper Room*, in the pages of *The Runner's Bible*, in Oxford Group writings, and in much of the Christian literature early AAs read with regularity. Many of these writings cite the correlative verses in James. And those of you who are steeped in A.A. sayings and thought should readily recognize the parallels.

A Review of the Bible's Book of James as It Reached A.A.

Both Bill W. and Dr. Bob stated many times that Jesus' Sermon on the Mount contained the underlying philosophy of A.A. Furthermore, our research has demonstrated how many words, phrases, and ideas in A.A. were borrowed from that Sermon. However, of probably much greater importance (than the Sermon) in the day-by-day thinking of early A.A., was the Book of James. It was much studied by A.A.'s co-founders. Quotes and ideas from the Apostle James can be found throughout the Big Book and in A.A. literature. As shown, the Book of James was considered so important that many favored calling the A.A. fellowship the "James Club." *DR. BOB and the Good Oldtimers,* p. 71; *Pass It On,* p. 147. And even the most fundamental phrases in A.A., such as "It Works" and Bill Wilson''s own "Works Publishing Company" (which published the First Edition of the Big Book), probably have their origin in the "Faith without works is dead" phrases in the Book of James See: Nell Wing, *Grateful to Have Been There,* pp. 70-71.

Let's therefore undertake a review the Book of James, chapter by chapter, and verse by verse. As we do so, we will point to traces of that book which we believe can be found in, or probably influenced the text of, the Big Book. At the outset, we would report that as our research into the Biblical roots of A.A. has progressed, so has our understanding of some root sources that previously went unnoticed.

Now let's look at the chapters in James—one by one.

James Chapter 1

Patience. Chapter One is not the only chapter in the Book of James which mentions patience. Nor is it the only portion of the Bible that stresses patience. But we've noted that James was a favored Biblical source in early A.A., and James 1:3-4 do state:

> Knowing *this,* that the trying of your faith worketh patience. But let patience have *her* perfect work, that ye may be perfect and entire, wanting nothing.

Patience certainly wound up as one of the most frequently mentioned spiritual principles in the Big Book (Fourth Ed., pp. 67, 70, 83, 111, 118, 163). And patience figured heavily as a *sine qua non* for application of the three absolutely essential beginning points for the Akron newcomer: Patience in overcoming the throes of acute withdrawal. Patience in dealing with the roller-coaster days of delayed withdrawal. And, of course, patience in recognizing that there is no progress toward a cure that does not necessitate patience in resisting temptation and remaining abstinent.

Asking wisdom of God with unwavering believing. James 1:5-8 state:

> If any of you lack wisdom, let him ask of God, that giveth to all *men* liberally, and upbraideth not; and it shall be given him.
>
> But let him ask in faith, nothing wavering. For he that wavereth is like a wave of the sea driven with the wind and tossed.

> For let not that man think that he shall receive anything of the Lord. A double minded man *is* unstable in all his ways.

Asking for God's direction and strength and receiving "Guidance" from Him, are major themes in both the Old and New Testaments. They were important Oxford Group ideas as well. We therefore discussed them at length in our titles on the Oxford Group and on Anne Smith's spiritual journal. Certainly the Big Book, including the Eleventh Step itself, is filled with such Guidance concepts (Fourth Ed., pp.13, 46, 49, 62-63, 69-70, 76, 79-80, 83, 84-88, 100, 117, 120, 124, 158, 164). Seeking God's guidance, wisdom, and strength—without giving in to doubt or faltering—is vital in resisting temptation and finding a safe and Godly way out and through the shoals.

Resisting temptation. It should surprise no one that AAs of yesteryear and of today are interested in resisting temptation, and having the power to do that——that power being the power of God. James 1:12-16 state:

> Blessed is the man that endureth temptation: for when he is tried, he shall receive the crown of life, which the Lord hath promised to those that love him.
>
> Let no man say when he is tempted, I am tempted of God: for God cannot be tempted with evil, neither tempteth he any man:
>
> But every man is tempted when he is drawn away of his own lust and enticed.
>
> Then when lust hath conceived, it bringeth forth sin: and sin, when it is finished, bringeth forth death.
>
> Do not err, my beloved brethren.
> Patient, relentless, resistance to temptation accompanied by action in obedience to God's wisdom and guidance were keys to cure.

A special note on resisting temptation (with God's help), being cured, and remaining cured.

My personal view is that the foregoing verses in James 1:12-16, offer much insight into the *cure* of alcoholism and other life-controlling afflictions as early AAs saw the solution when they so often claimed they were "cured." See Dick B., *Cured: Proven Help for Alcoholics and Addicts*, and Richard K. *So You Think that Drunks Cannot Be Cured*.

Man's job is to resist the devil--says James in one verse. Man is to endure temptation when he is tried, says another. When he is tempted, he cannot blame the temptation on God--who cannot be tempted and does not tempt. Man can be tempted by being drawn away of his own lust and enticed. James 3:15-16 speaks of a "wisdom [that] descendeth not from above, but is earthly, sensual, and devilish." And, says James, when the enticement produces lustful [and excessive] thoughts and behavior [such as getting drunk and drunkenness], it can and should be recognized as sin, and sin as the producer of death.

For the "real" alcoholic (who is willing to go to any lengths to beat alcohol), the "devilish," tempting thoughts must be resisted and expelled. The early A.A. prescription required much more than mere abstinence from drinking and going to 12 Step meetings. In fact there were no steps and were no meetings. That's not in the Book of James. The enjoined failure to resist occured when a man failed to submit to God, resist the devil, humble himself in the sight of God, and appropriately believe to be lifted up and out by his Creator.

Thus 2 Corinthians 10:5 calls for casting down human reasoning and "every high thing that exalteth itself against the knowledge of God, and bringing into captivity every thought to the obedience of Christ."

We are the ones who are to control the thoughts. God provides the strength. 1 Corinthians 10:13 points out:

> There hath no temptation taken you but such as is common to man; but God is faithful, who will not suffer you to be tempted above that ye are able; but will with the temptation also make a way to escape, that ye may be able to bear it.

> To be "cured" of what Dr. Bob called the curse of alcoholism, I believe, we need to recognize that the temptation to disobey

God is common and, as Paul wrote, "Now, if I do that I would not, it is no more I that do it, but sin that dwelleth in me. I find then a law, that, when I would do good, evil is present with me" (Romans 7:20-21).

The serpent tempted Eve to disobey God, and she did—reaping spiritual death for herself and Adam, who joined her in disobedience (Genesis 2:16-3:24; Romans 5:12-21). The devil tempted Jesus for forty days; but Jesus resisted each offer and challenge from the devil by standing on God's Word and quoting it to the devil (Luke 4:1-13)—who, by the way, earned a title as "the tempter" (1 Thessalonians 3:5). And the Lord's Prayer asks that God lead no disciples to be tempted, but rather that He deliver them from evil (Matthew 6:13).

In many verses of the Bible, God makes it clear that His will is against drunkenness (*e.g.*: Galatians 5:21). In Ephesians 5:18, He commands: "And be not drunk with wine, wherein is excess." Drunkenness from "excessive" drinking is, according to God's admonition, to be abhorred. Compare the comments in Jerry G. Dunn, *God is for the Alcoholic* Chicago: Moody Press, 1965, pp. 70-72, with those in Philip Tate. Alcohol: *How To Give It Up and Be Glad You Did.* AZ: See Sharp Press, 1997.

Jerry Dunn makes the case that the Bible doesn't tell anyone *not* to drink but that it does establish that *drunkenness* is sin. According to Dunn, there is also a strong case that a Christian should abstain; but that is a matter of choice. Tate, on the other hand, contends that you can give up drinking by using rational thinking—without resorting to A.A. or religion. Again, a case is made for *choice* and how to implement it. But recognize that despite the fact that these two writers come from completely different starting points, both make the case for choice and how to implement it.

Dr. Bob took several stern, simple positions about the alcoholic, abstinence, temptation, and drinking. These views had nothing to do with cure or no cure. They had to do with what the real alcoholic inevitably does after the first drink. *DR. BOB*, tells us:

Doc would hit first with the medical facts. . . . He also emphasized that it was a *fatal* illness and that the only way a man could recover from it—or rather not die from it—was not to take a drink to start with. That was the basis of the whole thing. In turn, we were pounding it into each other. After this, we got to the spiritual part (p. 113)

He'd say, [Dr. Bob would say:] Stay away from that place [Stone's grill with a back bar]. They have got nothing in there that you can't get somewhere else, whether it's food, cigarettes, or a Coke. Remembering his own disastrous trip to Atlantic City and Bill's experiment with keeping liquor on the sideboard to prove it was no longer a temptation, Dr. Bob advocated that members stay in dry places whenever possible. "You don't ask the Lord not to lead you into temptation, then turn around and walk right into it," he said (p. 281)

He [Dr. Bob] told me that before I could be honest with him or my sponsor or anyone else, I had to "get honest with that joker in the glass. . . . When you shave tomorrow, get honest with the man who looks back at you from the looking glass." Dr. Bob said that even then, it wasn't "Easy Does It" for him. "In the morning, when I get up and put my feet on the cold floor. . . I have a battle all day to stay away from that drink. You know, Dan, there were times in the early days of Alcoholics Anonymous when I passed those saloons that I had to pull my car over to the side of the curb and say a prayer" (p. 282)

Another thing Dr. Bob put quite simply: "The first one will get you." According to John R., he kept repeating that (p. 227).

Dr. Bob was stressing willpower, abstinence, and resisting temptation—not the "powerless" position incorporated in later A.A. thinking and writing.

Was Dr. Bob cured?

You decide: He never took a drink after June 10, 1935 (the agreed date of his sobriety). He had a strong relationship with God, and practiced strong fellowship with God. Having been burned once in Atlantic City at the beginning, he consistently stayed away from temptation and that first drink. He spent the happiest years of his life, with wife and family, after he quit drinking for good. Sounds to me like he was cured and enjoying an abundant spiritual life. And that's what we are shooting for.

The original Akron program insisted emphatically that "An alcoholic must realize that he is an alcoholic, incurable from a medical viewpoint, and that he must never again drink anything with alcohol in it. . . . [he must] want to stop drinking permanently." *DR. BOB*, p. 131. That means, concerning temptation, that any lingering thoughts about letting temptation make a nest in our mind and motivate our behavior must be, and can be, cast out if our behavior is to conform with God's will (2 Corinthians 10:5). Tempting thoughts need to be resisted. They need to be expelled. And we need to believe what God says in the Book of James—we are to submit ourselves to God; resist the devil; and be assured by God own Word and declaration that the devil *will* flee. And he does! We need to believe that God will lift us up and out. We need to believe that we can escape the net and bear the temptation with the help of our faithful Creator.

Willpower: Resisting temptation certainly requires willpower, believing, praying, changing behavior, changing ideas, changing habits, changing hobbies, changing cronies, and changing hangouts. See some of the suggestions about sound thinking and actions that are made by the "rational recovery" folks. Tate, *How to Give it Up*. Facing up to, and resisting, temptation is not a matter of bravado. People who are allergic to strawberries shouldn't eat strawberries. They don't need to be brave, just abstinent. People who get a bad, stinging rash from touching nettles shouldn't touch nettles. They don't need to be brave— just willful about avoidance. People who break out in blisters when they brush against poison oak should stay away from poison oak. Again, no bravery involved—just sane thinking and sane actions. It's not a question of "cure" or "no cure;" "recovered" or "not recovered;" a "daily reprieve or no daily reprieve." Fear or no fear, abstinence involves the will to be and become sufficiently sane in thinking that you don't walk into the lair of a hungry, ferocious, roaring lion. Expecting peace, quiet, safety, and joy.

One seemingly curious A.A. motto is "Think. Think. Think." And years back, I wondered what it meant. I asked around the fellowship and got no answer. I'm not sure anyone knows, but Joe McQ., of Big Book Seminar repute, suggested to me during a visit with him in Little Rock that it means: "Use your head."

You are the one who has to decide, "I quit." You are the one who has to be determined to "do anything to stay sober." You are the one who has to reject the tempting thoughts—to abstain, to reach out for help, to resist, and to ask for God's help. As Bill Wilson often said, A.A. has no monopoly on God. Nor does it offer the only way to get sober. Nor does it reject the idea that you may think you can later "drink like a gentleman." It simply suggests a way out of that thinking.

You can be cured of the curse of alcoholism, but you are nuts for sure if you start drinking and think that the tempter, the temptation, and the return of all the old stuff will not get you. Sanely thinking about what excessive drinking did to you can be an instrument of success. Failure to think that way can be an assurance of failure. God's help, the "use of your head," the application of willpower, a strong belief in God's power, a real request to God for His help, and the resolute changing of your old behavior, can and do produce success. These elements have for me. They did for the Pioneers. And the Pioneers tried to tell us that these suggested ideas could assure a cure for you.

Every good and perfect gift comes from God, the Father of lights.
James 1:17 states:

> Every good gift and every perfect gift is from above, and cometh down from The Father of lights, with whom is no variableness, neither shadow of turning.

Bill seemed to be referring to this verse when he wrote on page 14 of *Alcoholics Anonymous*, 4th ed.:

> I must turn in all things to the Father of Light [sic] who presides over us all [Alcoholics Anonymous, 1st ed., correctly says "the Father of Lights," p. 23.]

Bill made the same reference to our Creator, the Father of lights, who presides over us all, in Appendix I of *Alcoholics Anonymous*, 4th ed.:

> This to the end that our great blessings may never spoil us; that we shall forever live in thankful contemplation of Him who presides over us all. p. 566.

The "Him" who presides over us all was, of course, James 1:17's "Father of lights"--the Creator, Yahweh, our one true living God.

There are devilish, tempting thoughts available for your choice any time. There are also unchanging good and perfect thoughts from Yahweh our God. We are the ones to choose which we will allow to guide our actions.

Let every man be slow to speak, slow to wrath. James 1:19-20 state:

> Wherefore, my beloved brethren, let every man be swift to hear, slow to speak, slow to wrath: For the wrath of man worketh not the righteousness of God.

This same verse is quoted in *The Runner's Bible* and seems quite relevant to the Big Book's injunction, "If we were to live, we had to be free of anger. . . . God save me from being angry" (Fourth Edition, pp. 66-67).

The angry person frequently lets his guard down. He yields to temptation and often rejects reasonable thinking. The angry person is beginning with a focus on devilish thoughts, instead of those which, as James puts it, come down from above.

Be ye doers of the word, and not hearers only. James 1:21-22 state:

> Wherefore lay apart all filthiness and superfluity of naughtiness, and receive with meekness the engrafted word, which is able to save your souls.
>
> But be ye doers of the word, and not hearers only, deceiving your own selves.

Reverend Sam Shoemaker, whom Bill W. called an A.A. co-founder, made this comment on the foregoing:

> I think St. James's meaning is made much clearer in Dr. Moffatt's translation, "Act on the Word, instead of merely listening to it." Try it out in experiment, and prove it by its results——otherwise you only fool yourself into believing that you have the heart of religion when you haven't. Shoemaker, *The Gospel According to You,* pp. 44-55.

In the same chapter, Shoemaker also pointed out that prayer is often more a struggle to find God than the enjoyment of Him and cooperation with His will. He added that "God is and is a Rewarder of them that seek Him." See Shoemaker, *The Gospel According to You,* p. 47; and Hebrews 11:6.

I have not found specific or similar language to that of James 1:21-22 in the Big Book; but A.A. declares over and over that A.A. is a program of *action,* that probably no human power can relieve a person of his alcoholism, and "That God could and would if He were *sought"* (4the ed., p. 60, emphasis added). A.A.'s program emphasizes action in the experiment of faith it adopted from John 7:17——*seeking* God by *following* the path that leads to a relationship with God. James 1:22 enjoins *doing* God's will as expressed in His Word——not merely listening to it. James was an Akron favorite. Shoemaker was a Wilson favorite. "Faith without works" was a Big Book favorite; and it therefore seems quite reasonable to believe, and altogether possible, that A.A.'s emphasis on *action* might well have derived largely from James 1:21-22.

A "hearer" may very well receive and even consider acting on a siren call. A "doer" has heard the Word, has learned the difference between devilish calls and calls from God; and, as a doer of the Word, he acts on the latter.

Pure religion and undefiled before God . . . to visit the fatherless and widows in their affliction. *James* 1:27 states:

> Pure religion and undefiled before God and the Father is this, To visit the fatherless and widows in their affliction, *and* to keep oneself unspotted from the world.

At the very least, this verse bespeaks unselfishness and helpfulness to others which were cardinal A.A. principles--particularly the principles embodied in Step Twelve. In fact, that's the point made in one of early A.A.'s pamphlets:

> And all we need to do in the St. James passage is to substitute the word "Alcoholic" for "Fatherless and Widows" and we have Step Twelve. *Spiritual Milestones*, AA of Akron, pp. 12-13.

AAs pledge themselves to obey and do God's will. They are also taught to strengthen their obedience with Godly deeds that will also remind them of the deadly results that come from yielding to temptation. Their unique method is through helping other afflicted drunks and trying to keep their own houses clean.

James Chapter 2

Chapter Two of the Book of James may have made two direct and major contributions to the language of the Big Book and also to A.A.'s philosophy. Those two contributions were "Love thy neighbor as thyself" and "Faith without works is dead."

Love thy neighbor as thyself. James 2:8 states:

> If ye fulfill the royal law according to the scripture, Thou shalt love thy neighbor as thyself, ye do well.

This commandment to "Love thy neighbor" exists in other parts of both the Old and New Testaments. Thus, when the Big Book incorporated this phrase, there is no assurance that the quote is from James rather than from another Bible verse to the same effect (*e.g.*, Rom. 13:9; Gal. 5:14). But the Big Book certainly does state:

> Then you will know what it means to give of yourself that others may survive and rediscover life. You will learn the full meaning of "Love thy neighbor as thyself" (Fourth ed., p. 153).

Such Big Book remarks point out to the recovered alcoholic that the spiritual objective of loving his neighbor can certainly be realized by the helping act.

The Book of James is very probably the specific source of this Biblical quote since Dr. Bob, early AAs, and Bill Wilson himself spoke with such frequency about "love" and tolerance as the code of A.A. *and* the Book of James as AAs' favorite book.

Faith without works is dead. Said to be the favorite verse of Anne Smith and perhaps the origin of many expressions in A.A. concerning "works," this sentence, or variations of it, appears several times in Chapter Two of the Book of James. For example, James 2:20 states:

> But wilt thou know, 0 vain man, that faith without works is dead?

"Faith without works" as a phrase, and as an A.A. "action" concept, is quoted or referred to many times in the Big Book (4th ed., pp. 14-15, 76, 88, 93, 97). A.A.'s original Oxford Group connection also put emphasis on these James verses concerning the importance of witnessing and "sharing for witness" as they called it. And sometimes,

I believe, A.A. today has put far too much emphasis on "works" (often calling it "service") yet ignored and forgotten the "faith" part. The "faith" of pioneer A.A. is the faith of Jesus Christ. Galatians 2:16 says:

> Knowing that a man is not justified by the works of the law, but by the faith of Jesus Christ, even we have believed in Jesus Christ, that we might be justified by the faith of Christ, and not by the works of the law: for by the works of the law shall no flesh be justified.

As Galatians explains, the Bible is not talking about faith in terms of words or acts of kindness and good deeds. The empowering faith—the acquittal of guilt—comes by grace, and not by what man has observed or done. It comes because God blesses His kids with unearned rewards, not because they placed their faith in His words and prescribed works, but because they received their faith, obeyed despite their words and works, but were justified because of what their Lord Jesus Christ and his faith had done for them.

Helping Others. It hardly requires citation or documentation to state that A.A.'s cardinal objective is to help others. Specifically, other drunks who reach out for help. Early on, the Big Book states, "Our very lives, as ex-problem drinkers, depend upon our constant thought of others and how we may help meet their needs" (Fourth ed., p. 20). Later, it continues at page 89:

> Practical experience shows that nothing will so much insure immunity from drinking as intensive work with other alcoholics. It works when other activities fail. This is our *twelfth suggestion*: Carry this message to other alcoholics! You can help when no one else can. You can secure their confidence when others fail.

The basic spiritual backdrop is underlined in Chapter 2 of James. That chapter begins by talking of the love of God which decrees Godly works, beginning with verses 1 to 7 which say:

> My brethren, have not the faith of our Lord Jesus Christ, the Lord of glory, with respect of persons. For if there come unto your assembly a man with a gold ring, in goodly apparel, and

there come in also a poor man in vile raiment; And ye have respect to him that weareth the gay clothing, and say unto him, Sit thou here in a good place; and say to the poor, Stand thou there, or sit here under my footstool: Are ye not then partial in yourselves, and are become judges of evil thoughts? Hearken, my beloved brethren, Hath not God chosen the poor of this world rich in faith, and heirs of the kingdom which he hath promised to them that love him? But ye have despised the poor. Do not rich men oppress you, and draw you before the judgment seats? Do not they blaspheme that worthy name by the which ye are called?

James 2:15-16 state this principle of making unconditional, non-discriminating good deeds very well:

If a brother or sister be naked, and destitute of daily food, And one of you say unto them, Depart in peace, be ye warmed and filled; notwithstanding ye give them not those things which are needful to the body; what doth it profit? Even so, faith, if it hath not works, is dead, being alone.

And every alcoholic who has helped one of his miserable, suffering, destitute brothers in need will, I believe, instantly relate to those verses and hence to the importance the early AAs attached to James itself.

The Ten Commandments. Again! James 2:10-11 state:

For whosoever shall keep the whole law, and yet offend in one *point,* he is guilty of all. For he that said, Do not commit adultery, said also, Do not kill. Now if thou commit no adultery, yet if thou kill, thou art become a transgressor of the law.

Believers are not accorded the liberty of picking and choosing which of God's commandments are acceptable and worthy of their attention. They are told to obey all. Whatever one may think is representative of, or acceptable in today's A.A., he will find language about and references to the Ten Commandments with great frequency in *early*

A.A. You will see more of this same point in our review of the Sermon on the Mount.

James Chapter 3

Taming the tongue. In his Farewell Address to A.A., Dr. Bob said:

> Let us also remember to guard that erring member the tongue, and if we must use it, let's use it with kindness and consideration and tolerance. *DR. BOB and the Good Oldtimers,* p. 338.

A major portion of James chapter 3 is devoted to the trouble that can be caused by an untamed tongue. Following are a few verses emphasizing the point:

> Even so the tongue is a little member and boasteth great things.
> Behold, how great a matter a little fire kindleth! And the tongue is a fire, a world of iniquity; so is the tongue among our members that it defileth the whole body, and setteth on fire the course of nature; and it is set on fire of hell.
> But the tongue can no man tame; it is an unruly evil, full of deadly poison. Out of the same mouth proceedeth blessing and cursing. My brethren, these things ought not to be (James 3:5, 6, 8, 10)

These verses are not quoted in the Big Book. But Anne Smith referred to them frequently in her journal, as did other A.A. roots sources. Dick B., *Anne Smith"s Journal,* pp. 28, 44, 76, 77; Holm, *The Runner"s Bible,* p. 68. But, in paraphrasing those verses, Dr. Bob seemed to be speaking of the necessity for tolerance, courtesy, consideration, and kindness in our speech and actions. James makes clear that good *conversation* should be a focus—conversation, we believe, that is laced with consideration, kindness, and tolerance (See James 3:13). And these latter principles *are* very much in evidence in the Big Book (4th ed., pp. 67, 69-70, 83-84, 97, 118, 125, 135).

Outspoken fiery language incites untoward action and diminishes sound reasoning. God opposes it. And man's obedience to God's injunctions reminds that God blesses those who obey.

Avoidance of envy, strife, and lying. James 3:14-16 proclaim that a heart filled with envy, strife, and lies has not received *that* kind of "wisdom" from God, but rather from devilish sources. The verses state:

> But if ye have bitter envying and strife in your hearts; glory not, and lie not against the truth.
>
> This wisdom descendeth not from above, but is earthly, sensual, devilish.
>
> For where envying and strife is, there is confusion and every evil work

.

"Envy" is not as much decried in the Big Book as jealousy; but a more modern translation of these King James verses equates "envy" *with "jealousy." The Revised English Bible, New Testament*, p, 208. And the Big Book most assuredly condemns jealously (4th ed., pp. 37, 69, 82, 100, 119, 145, 161). In fact, the Big Book states as to jealousy *and* envy:

> Keep it always in sight that we are dealing with that most terrible human emotion——jealousy (p. 82).
>
> The greatest enemies of us alcoholics are resentment, jealousy, envy, frustration, and fear (p. 145).

Again these "enemies" in action violate God's rules. They replace Godly wisdom with devilish thinking. They open the door to many and all the devilish behaviors that descend from devilish sources.

And as to strife, the Big Book states:

> After all, our problems were of our own making. Bottles were only a symbol. Besides, we have stopped fighting anybody or anything. We have to (4th ed., p. 103)!

James 3:17-18 talk much about making peace and the fruit of righteousness being sown in peace of them that make peace.

As seen in the quote from James 3:14, lying and dishonesty are also declared to be devilish; and one should note and compare the Big Book's frequent emphasis on grasping and developing a manner of living which "demands rigorous honesty" (4th ed., p. 58). As to all the verses in James 3:14-16, however, there is little certainty that these particular verses were an exclusive or even major source for the Big Books condemnation of envy, jealousy, strife, and dishonesty because all these traits are stated to be objectionable by many other parts of the Bible. They are resolutely condemned in God's Word.

James Chapter 4:

Asking amiss for selfish ends. A.A.'s writings have much to say about overcoming selfishness and self-centeredness. But the following in James 4:3 particularly eschews determined selfishness in prayer:

> Ye ask, and receive not, because ye ask amiss, that ye may consume it upon your lusts.

Several Christian A.A. sources that were favorites of Dr. Bob's discuss this verse at length. And the Big Book authors may therefore have borrowed from James 4:3, in this statement:

> We ask especially for freedom from self-will, and are careful to make no request for ourselves only. We may ask for ourselves, however, if others will be helped. We are careful never to pray for our own selfish ends. Many of us have wasted a lot of time doing that and it doesn't work (Big Book, 4th ed., p. 87).

Neither does failure to ask in accordance with God's will (See 1 John 5:14-15).

Humility. The Book of James has no corner on the Biblical injunction to be humble. But the importance of James, and the remarks of Reverend Samuel Shoemaker (quoted under Item 3 immediately below) suggest that the following verses from James may have been a source of the Big Book's frequent mention of humility. James 4:7, 10 state:

> Submit yourselves therefore to God. Resist the devil, and he will flee from you.
>
> Humble yourselves in the sight of the Lord, and he shall lift you up.

God requires that His will be sought, and He promises rewards to those who seek it.

The Big Book's Fourth Edition is filled with exhortations to be humble, with stress on humbling one's self before God, and with suggestions for humbly asking His help. Examples include:

> There I humbly offered myself to God, as I understood Him, to do with me as He would (p. 13).
>
> He humbly offered himself to his Maker——then he knew (p. 57).
>
> Just to the extent that we do as we think He would have us, and humbly rely on Him, does He enable us to match calamity with serenity (p. 68).
>
> We constantly remind ourselves we are no longer running the show, humbly saying to ourselves many times each day "Thy will be done" (pp. 87-88).

Trusting God and cleaning house. James 4:8 states:

> Draw nigh to God, and he will draw nigh to you. Cleanse your hands, ye sinners; and purify your hearts, ye double minded.

The Big Book says on page 98 of the Fourth Edition:

> Burn the idea into the consciousness of every man that he can get well regardless of anyone. The only condition is that he trust in God and clean house.

And, in language closely paralleling that in James 4:8, the Big Book says further that one can establish conscious companionship with God by simply, honestly, and humbly seeking and drawing near to Him:

> He has come to all who have honestly sought Him. When we drew near to Him He disclosed Himself to us (page 57)

In Step Seven, the Big Book relates "cleaning house" of one's character defects to "humbly asking" God to remove them. The foregoing verses in James, which speak of drawing near to God, cleansing our hearts, humbling ourselves in His sight, and then being "lifted" up by God, appear to have been directly involved in framing the Big Book's Seventh Step language. In fact, many years after the Big Book was written, Sam Shoemaker thus clarified his understanding of the Seventh Step, in a 1964 issue of the *AA Grapevine*:

> Sins get entangled deep within us, as some roots of a tree, and do not easily come loose. We need help, grace, the lift of a kind of divine derrick Shoemaker, "Those Twelve Steps as I Understand Them"; *Volume II, Best of the Grapevine*, p. 130.

All such verses, Big Book remarks, and statements by Sam Shoemaker illustrate that the elimination of all sins—including yielding to temptation—are involved in changing. It is not just the effort of man that solves the problem. It is God's help that saves the day.

Taking your own inventory. James 4:11-12 state:

> Speak not evil one of another, brethren. He that speaketh evil of *his* brother, and judgeth his brother, speaketh evil of the

law, and judgeth the law: but if thou judge the law, thou art not a doer of the law, but a judge.

There is one lawgiver, who is able to save and to destroy: who art thou that judgest another?

Later, we discuss the importance of A.A.'s Fourth Step inventory process as it derives from relevant verses in the Sermon on the Mount--which were often quoted by Oxford Group people and by Anne Smith (See Matt. 7:1-5). But the Big Book places special emphasis on this inventory process, suggesting that we examine all biblical sources for the Big Book's talk of: (1) looking "for our own mistakes," (2) asking "Where were we to blame," and (3) realizing, "The inventory was ours, not the other man's." Considering the importance to AAs of the Book of James and its insights, the foregoing James verses in James 4:11-12 probably also had an impact on the A.A. idea of avoiding judgment of another and focusing on an examination of one's own conduct when it comes to wrongdoing.

James Chapter 5

Patience. We discussed A.A.'s "patience principle" as having probably derived from James, Chapter One. As we said, however, additional stress on patience can be found in James 5:7, 8, 10, 11. There is to be patience in (a) Recognizing and enduring temptation. (b) Seeking God's help when temptation arises. (c) Resisting the "tempter"—knowing that he will yield to the power of God and flee. That's the simple answer James offers the believer.

Grudges (covered in A.A.'s 4th Step resentment inventory process). James 5:9 reads:

Grudge not one against another, brethren, lest ye be condemned; behold, the judge standeth before the door.

A major portion of the Big Book's Fourth Step discussion is devoted to resentment, about which page 64 says:

Resentment is the "number one" offender. It destroys more alcoholics than anything else. From it stem all forms of spiritual disease.

In the context of victorious living, this variety of sin is just another example of where the believer is to give place to Godly thoughts and actions instead of yielding to devilish ones.

The Big Book suggests putting resentments *on paper*—making a *"grudge list"* (pp. 64-65). Oxford Group spokesman Ebenezer Macmillan wrote at length in his title *Seeking and Finding* about eliminating resentments, hatred, or the *"grudge"* that "blocks God out effectively." Rev. Sam Shoemaker also specified "grudges" as one of the "sins" to be examined in an inventory of self. Shoemaker, *Twice-Born Ministers*, p. 182. The Big Book suggests listing resentments or "grudges" as one of the four major "character defects" which block us from God; and it seems quite possible that the "grudge" language in the Big Book was influenced by James, and perhaps specifically by James 5:9.

Asking God's forgiveness for sins. Here and elsewhere in the Bible, we find an answer to the hopelessness and despair which so often beset the alcoholic. The Word of God offers relief to the repentant sinner—not just endless condemnation. We repeat James 5:15, which was partially quoted above. The entire verse says:

> And the prayer of faith shall save the sick, and the Lord shall raise him up; and if he have committed sins, they shall be forgiven him.

Compare the following Big Book statements about asking God''s forgiveness when we fall short:

> If we are sorry for what we have done, and have the honest desire to let God take us to better things, we believe we will be forgiven and will have learned our lesson (4th ed, p. 70).

> When we retire at night, we constructively review our day. . . . After making our review, we ask God's forgiveness and inquire what corrective measures should be taken (4th ed., p. 86).

The foregoing Big Book quotes seem to demonstrate Bill Wilson's view that, even after their initial surrender, wrongdoers may continue sinning and therefore may still, in A.A.'s view (and with certainly the Bible's assurance), seek and receive God's forgiveness for shortcomings indulged after the initial surrender. Here again, James has no corner on the statement that God makes it possible, through forgiveness, for a believer to regain fellowship with Him. The following in 1 John 1:9 may also have been a source of such Big Book ideas:

> If we confess our sins, he is faithful and just to forgive us *our* sins, and to cleanse us from all unrighteousness.

We will further discuss forgiveness in connection with the Sermon on the Mount. It is fair to say, however, that the Book of James, 1 John, or Matthew could each, or all, have been the basis for the Big Book forgiveness concept.

Confess your sins one to another. It has often been noted that *both* the Oxford Group concept of sharing by confession *and* Step Five in the Big Book were derived from James 5:16:

> Confess your faults one to another, and pray for one another, that ye may be healed.

Of much more significance than "sharing by confession" and the source of Step Five is the direct patterning of Akron's "real surrenders" on this verse and those surrounding it. Akron brothers did pray for the new man. First, they brought him to Christ; they prayed for him as he accepted Christ and uttered with them his own prayers that alcohol be taken out of his life, that he be cured, and that he be enabled to live by the principles of Christ. The objective was to have him become a Christian—then relying on the power and guidance of

God for cure and a life lived in obedience to the cardinal doctrines of Christ.

The Roman Catholic Church had problems with this interpretation of James. It talked irrelevantly and with condemnation about "open confessions" in the Oxford Group and then relevantly about that church's insistence that confessions be made to a priest—not a group of "elders."

Effectual, fervent prayer works. James 5:16 states:

> The effectual fervent prayer of a righteous man availeth much.

A.A.'s Big Book Fourth Edition says:

> Step Eleven suggests prayer and meditation. We shouldn't be shy on this matter of prayer. Better men than we are using it constantly. It works, if we have the proper attitude and work at it.

James 5:16 could well have been a major, albeit unacknowledged, basis for the Big Book comments on the effectiveness of prayer.

Anointing with oil and effecting healings through prayer by elders. See James 5:13-16.

One A.A. writer, who was sponsored by the venerable old-timer Clarence Snyder, has repeatedly suggested that, in their "surrenders," early AAs almost literally followed the foregoing verses from James. Many others (seven that I have personally interviewed—Berry W., Grace S., Steve F., John S., Dick B., Dale M., and Jack R.) who also were sponsored by Clarence Snyder, have stated emphatically that this contention is in error. In fact, A.A. old-timer Larry Bauer from Ohio both wrote and phoned me shortly before his death to say that he was quite familiar with the Akron surrenders, that he had been taken upstairs and was there born again, but that there had been *no anointing with oil*. Before we leave the Book of James, however, several comments should be made about surrenders, the Akron prayers, and the question of anointing.

First, there seems little confirmation of the story by one of Clarence Snyder's sponsees that Dr. Bob, T. Henry Williams, and the Akron pioneers took a newcomer "upstairs," had him "surrender" to Christ, prayed for him and with him, and anointed him with oil. The oil part has simply not been proven to my satisfaction in view of the fact that six of Clarence Snyder's presently living sponsees have told me personally that they knew of no anointing as they were taken through surrenders and later the Steps or nor had they heard history such an account from Clarence.

Second, in preparing my biography of the role of Clarence and his wife Grace in A.A., I spent a week in company with my son Ken at Grace's home at Jacksonville, Florida. And I think it is fair to say that there is nothing about Clarence's ministry and practices that was not covered with Grace. See Dick B., *That Amazing Grace*. Grace talked at length about what Clarence told her about the pioneer program, the surrenders, the prayers "upstairs," and how Clarence had taken people through the Steps for years. Dick B., *That Amazing Grace*, pp. 6, 27. But I can't recall Grace's mentioning anointing with oil by the pioneers though she and Clarence practiced this in their healing work and in the "prayer and praise" segments of their spiritual retreats, after the retreat itself had concluded. See particularly Dick B., *That Amazing Grace, supra*, pp. 95-97, 101, 6, 27. To be sure, many of the elements of the James verses *were* followed by the pioneers—including those relating to confession, healing, and prayer.

Third, in his later years, Clarence Snyder had, as we've said, founded and conducted retreats for AAs and their families. Most are still being held. At these retreats, there is a "prayer and praise" session where there *is* anointing with oil and prayer for those in need. The sessions *follow* the close of the retreat itself. See *Our A.A. Legacy to the Faith Community: A Twelve-Step Guide for Those Who Want to Believe*. By Three Clarence Snyder Sponsee Oldt-timers and Their Wives. Compiled and Edited by Dick B. FL: Came to Believe Publications, 2005, pp. 99-100.

Finally, we make particular mention of the pioneer confession, prayer, healing, and anointing ideas in James because so many of the healing practices of the Christian church in the beginning and throughout later centuries did rely on the words of St. James and did heal with the laying on of hands and anointing with oil. There is an enormous amount of scholarly writing on James 5:16, confession, "Unction," prayer by the elders, and the laying on of hands in connection with Christian healing. These writings certainly did not all escape the notice and readings by Dr. Bob on Christian healing.

Probably the leading work on anointing and Scripture is F.W. Puller, *The Anointing of the Sick in Scripture and Tradition, with some Considerations on the Numbering of the Sacraments.* London: Society For Promoting Christian Knowledge, 1904. Others include Percy Dearmer, *Body and Soul: An Enquiry into the Effects of Religion upon Health, with a description of Christian Works of Healing From the New Testament to the Present Day.* London: Sir Isaac Pitman & Sons, Ltd., 1909), 217-255, 287-292, 396-400; J. R. Pridie, *The Church"s Ministry of Healing.* London: Society For Promoting Christian Knowledge, 1926, pp. 67-86, 110-114; George Gordon Dawson, *Healing: Pagan and Christian.* London: Society For Promoting Christian Knowledge, 1935, pp. 146-159; John Maillard, *Healing In The Name of Jesus.* London: Hodder & Stoughton, 1936, pp. 116, 283-284; James Moore Hickson, *Heal The Sick.* London: Methuen & Co., Ltd., 1924, pp. 252-269; and Evelyn Frost. *Christian Healing, 2d ed.* London: A. R. Mowbray & Co., Ltd., 1949, pp. 331-332.

These healing points are also extensively documented and discussed in the titles listed in the bibliographies in my recent works on healing and cure. See Dick B., *Cured: Proven Help for Alcoholics and Addicts.* Kihei, HI: Paradise Research Publications, Inc., 2003; *When Early AAs Were Cured. And Why.* Kihei, HI: Paradise Research Publications, Inc., 2003; and *God and Alcoholism: Our Growing Challenge in the 21st Century.* Kihei, HI: Paradise Research Publications, Inc., 2002. All the foregoing materials cast a new light on how and why early AAs all said they had been cured; that there was a cure for alcoholism; and that they had developed a cure.

Their belief in healing and cure was supported and fortified by nineteen centuries of Christian healing records.

There is newly confirmed early A.A. history of the bringing of newcomers to Christ, having them ask God to take alcohol out of their lives, and having them ask in Jesus' name for strength and guidance to live by His principles. See Mitchell K. *How It Worked.* NY: A.A. Big Book Study Group, 1999, pp. 58, 69-71, 139, 215-216; Clarence Snyder, *Going Through the Steps*. FL: Stephen Foreman, 1985; *Three Clarence Snyder Sponsees, Our A.A. Legacy.* There is also newly confirmed proof that Akron old timers prayed for and with the newcomer in their "surrenders"--asking God to heal, guide, and strengthen. There is a vast amount of newly gathered evidence of a decade of early A.A. cures in its first decade of existence. You can find the documentation and accounts of these facts in my titles cited immediately above; in Mitchell K.'s *How It Worked*, and also in several very recent titles by a prodigious writer and careful researcher new to our A.A. historian scene. See Richard K., *Separating Fact From Fiction: How Revisionists Have Led Our History Astray* Haverhill, MA: Golden Text Publishing Co., 2003; *So You Think Drunks Can"t Be Cured?* Haverhill, MA: Golden Text Publishing Co., 2003.

I believe all the foregoing historical facts are important. The convictions about "healing" and "cure" were so evident and strong in early A.A. And a return of healing emphasis--whatever the technique or Biblical authority--is urgently needed in today's recovery programs (particularly those being launched in the "faith based community" sector).

What These Historical Facts about A.A. and Its Roots in the Book of James Offer Believers and Others in A.A. Today

If you are going to invent gods, place your faith in meetings, concentrate on not drinking, ignore the need to change your life, fail to ask God's help and guidance, and reject prayers for genuine healing, then just forget the Book of James in A.A. today.

My premise is that the Word of God contains the Will of God. If you don't like the Bible, don't believe in God, don't want to hear about Jesus Christ, think A.A. is supposed to be irreligious, and want the easy way of attendance at meetings——often just "centers of self-centeredness," then you don't need James or even the Good Book itself. But James contains some powerful injunctions about walking God's way, rejecting temptation, resisting the tempter, and being cured——of any temptation, sickness, and addictive urges.

Principles from the Book of James you can take to the bank.

Here are some simple points from James in the Good Book that believers who qualify as "real" alcoholics, and others searching for God's truth, can grab for and cling to.

Abstain, abstain, abstain: Excessive drinking starts from temptation and is appropriately called in the Bible "sin."

Be patient in your walk with God.

Ask God's wisdom and guidance with unwavering belief in His goodness.

Reject temptation. That is your job. God doesn't tempt, but, according to James, the devil sure does.

Do what God says, don't just listen to the Word and remain passive.

Anger, envy, strife, criticism, and grudges are devilish in origin and results; and they disobey God's Commandments.

Remember that your faith in God's love and power is to be accompanied by deeds consistent with His will.

Remember that your erring tongue can harm and constitute real sinning, and that its utterances—to be appropriate—must be consistent with good works.

Don't complain about unanswered prayers until your prayers coincide with God's will.

Submit yourself to God. Resist the devil. Believe the devil will take a hike.

And he will.

Cleanse your hands.

If you draw near to God, He will draw near to you.

Humility in seeking God, is an essential to His lifting you up.

Openly place your faults on the table and eliminate them.

Ask other believers for their prayers.

Ask God in the name of Jesus Christ for healing and cure and for solutions to all your problems.

Expect and believe for deliverance.

The effectual fervent prayer of a believer pays off.

A Key from James that should be a major factor for believers in A.A. today

You should make every effort to recognize that the key to the early A.A. program was not drunkalogs. It was not meetings. It was not cleaning up a drunk. It was Christian fellowship and witnessing by those who had suffered from similar problems, by those who had followed the path known as the "way," by those who had been cured themselves, and by those who therefore were able to describe exactly how it had happened, what they had done, and how God had done for them what they could not do for themselves.

This process involved an understanding of several factors: The malady, the requirement of abstaining from temptation, the necessity for Christ, knowing the promises of God, relying on the power of God, and obeying God's will. And all had been covered in the Good Book and known for centuries before A.A.

The malady-drunkenness:

> Proverbs 23:29-35: "Who hath woe? . . . . They that tarry too long at the wine. . . . At the last it biteth like a serpent, and stingeth like an adder. . . ."

> Proverbs 31:4-6: "It is not for kings, O Lemuel, it is not for kings to drink wine; nor for princes strong drink: Lest they drink, and forget the law, and pervert the judgment of any of the afflicted. . . ."

> Galatians 5:19-21: "Now the works of the flesh are manifest. . . envyings, murders, drunkenness. . . . they which do such things shall not inherit the kingdom of God."

> Ephesians 5:18: "And be not drunk with wine, wherein is excess. . . ."

The solution-submission to God and resisting the devil:

> James 4:7-10: "Submit yourselves therefore to God. Resist the devil, and he will flee from you. . . . Cleanse your hands, ye sinners; and purify your hearts, ye double minded. . . . Humble yourselves in the sight of the Lord, and he shall lift you up."

The necessity for Christ and reliance on the promises of God:

> Acts 4:10-12: "Be it known to you all, and to all the people of Israel, that by the name of Jesus Christ of Nazareth, whom you crucified, whom God raised from the dead, even by him doth this man [the man previously lame from birth] stand here before you whole. . . . Neither is there salvation in any other; for there is none other name under heaven given among men, whereby we must be saved."

> Acts 2:38-39: ". . . Repent, and be baptized every one of you in the name of Jesus Christ for the remission of sins, and ye shall receive the gift of the Holy Ghost. For the promise is

unto you and to your children, and to all that are afar off, even as many as the Lord our God shall call."

Acts 2:1-9: "Now Peter and John went up together unto the temple at the hour of prayer, being the ninth hour. And a certain man lame from his mother's womb was carried, whom they laid daily at the gate of the temple which is called Beautiful, to ask alms of them that entered into the temple. Who seeing Peter and John about to go into the temple asked an alms. And Peter, fastening his eyes upon him with John, said, Look on us. And he gave heed unto them, expecting to receive something of them. Then Peter said, Silver and gold have I none; but such as I have give I thee: In the name of Jesus Christ of Nazareth rise up and walk. And he took him by the right hand, and lifted him up: and immediately his feet and ancle bones received strength. And he leaping up stood, and walked, and entered into the temple, walking, and leaping, and praising God: And all the people saw him walking and praising God."

The Power of God:

Ephesians 1:19: "And what is the exceeding greatness of his power to us-ward who believe, according to the working of his mighty power."

Obedience to God's will—walking in the Spirit, obeying unto righteousness, enduring temptation and resisting it, and keeping God's commandments:

Galatians 5:16: "This I say then, Walk in the Spirit, and ye shall not fulfill the lust of the flesh." [A choice!]

Romans 6:16: "Know ye not, that to whom ye yield yourselves servants to obey, his servants are ye to whom ye obey, whether of sin unto death or obedience unto righteousness." [A choice!]

James 1:12-16: "Blessed is the man that endureth temptation: for when he is tried, he shall receive the crown of life which the Lord hath promised to them that love him. . . .But every man is tempted, when he is drawn way of his own lust, and enticed. Then when lust hath conceived, it bringeth forth sin: and sin, when it is finished, bringeth forth death. Do not err, my beloved brethren." [A choice!]

Ecclesiastes 12:13: "Let us hear the conclusion of the whole matter: Fear God, and keep his commandments: for this is the whole duty of man." [A choice]

Our Study of the Sermon on the Mount

Early AAs Heard about It All the Time

The Sermon on the Mount had a unique history in early A.A. Both Bill Wilson and Dr. Bob said several times that Jesus' Sermon on the Mount contained the underlying philosophy of A.A. A.A.'s own literature reports: "He [Dr. Bob] cited the Sermon on the Mount as containing the underlying spiritual philosophy of A.A." *DR. BOB and the Good Oldtimers.* NY: Alcoholics Anonymous World Services, Inc., 1980, p. 228. Dr. Bob had no hesitancy about reading from the Bible and reading this Sermon from it at meetings. An A.A. *Grapevine* article states that at a meeting led by Dr. Bob, Dr. Bob "put his foot on the rung of a dining-room chair, identified himself as an alcoholic, and began reading the Sermon on the Mount." *DR. BOB,* p. 218. Dr. Bob pointed out that there were no twelve steps at the beginning, that "our stories didn't amount to anything to speak of," and that they [A.A.'s "older ones"] were "convinced that the answer to their problems was in the Good Book." *DR. BOB*, p. 96.

A.A. Old-timer Clarence Snyder pointed out as to Dr. Bob: "If someone asked him a question about the program, his usual response was: 'What does it say in the Good Book?'" *DR. BOB*, p. 144. Bob said quite clearly: "I didn't write the Twelve Steps. I had nothing to do with the writing of them" but that "We already had the basic ideas, though not in terse and tangible form. We got them as a result of our study of the Good Book." *DR. BOB*, pp. 96-97. Dr. Bob stressed over and over that the "the parts we found absolutely essential were" the Book of James, the Sermon on the Mount, and 1 Corinthians 13 *(e.g. DR. BOB*, p. 96). In the Foreword Dr. Bob's son "Smitty" wrote for

Good Book and The Big Book, "Smitty" pointed to the A.A. of James, the Sermon, and Corinthians; and I heard his statement at several large A.A. history meetings, t A.A.'s San Diego International Convention in 1995.

ᵣ⌐ᵤₙsee Clarence Snyder, got sober in February of 1938 and later became the AA with the greatest amount of sobriety. Clarence often echoed Dr. Bob's words about the Bible and the three essential parts. Also, in a talk given to AAs in Glenarden, Maryland, on August 8, 1981, Clarence said: "This program emanates from the Sermon on the Mount and the Book of James. If you want to know where this program came from, read the fifth, sixth, seventh chapters of Matthew. Study it over and over, and you'll see the whole program in there" (Glen Cove, NY: Glenn K. Audio Tape #2451).

Of course, the Lord's Prayer itself can be found in several of the Gospels and particularly in Jesus' sermon at Matthew 6:9-13. This prayer from the sermon was originally and frequently recited by the A.A. pioneers at the close of every meeting (*e.g.: DR. BOB, supra*, pp. 141, 148, 183, 261)—just as it was in the meetings of the Oxford Group, from which A.A. derived. And just as it still is in most A.A. meetings today.

Bill Wilson actually quoted from two parts of the sermon in the Big Book—though he never indicated his source. He borrowed the phrase "Thy will be done" [from Matthew 6:10] and partly quoted "Thou shalt love thy neighbor as thyself" from Matthew 5:43 (also found in many other places in the Bible—*e.g.*: Leviticus 19:18; Romans 13:9; Galatians 5:14; James 2:8).

Dr. Bob read and circulated among early AAs and their families a good many materials that discussed every facet of the Sermon—*e.g.: Studies in the Sermon on the Mount* by Oswald Chambers (London: Simpkin, Marshall, Ltd., n.d.); *The Christ of the Mount: A Working Philosophy of Life* by E. Stanley Jones (NY: The Abingdon Press, 1931); *The Sermon on the Mount* by Emmet Fox (NY: Harper & Row, 1934); *The Lord's Prayer and Other Talks on Prayer from The Camps Farthest Out* by Glenn Clark (MN: Macalester Park Publishing Co., 1932); and *I Will Lift Up Mine Eyes* by Glenn Clark (NY: Harper & Brothers, 1937). See Dick B. *Dr. Bob and His Library*, 3rd ed. (Kihei,

HI: Paradise Research Publications, Inc., 1998); *DR. BOB and the Good Oldtimers*, pp.310-311.

Many Oxford Group books discussed the sermon as did many of the daily devotionals the early AAs used—devotionals such as *The Upper Room* and *The Runner's Bible*. See DR. BOB, supra, pp. 71, 139, 151, 178, 220, 311 and, as to *The Runner's Bible, DR. BOB*, p. 293; *RHS*. NY: A.A. Grapevine, Inc., 1951, p. 34; Dick B., *Good Morning*, 2d ed., *Dr. Bob and His Library*, 3rd ed., and *The Books Early AAs Read for Spiritual Growth,* 7th ed.

The Actual Sermon on the Mount AAs Read
(Matthew Chapters 5-7)

This discussion will not deal with a particular book or commentary on Matthew chapters 5-7. It will focus on the verses in the Sermon on the Mount itself. For this Sermon, which Jesus delivered, was not the property of some present-day commentator or writer. The fact that Dr. Bob read the Matthew chapters *themselves,* as well as many interpretations of them, verifies the A.A. belief that the Sermon was one of the principles comprising "the common property of mankind," which Bill Wilson said the AAs had borrowed. And here are some major points that appear to have found their way from the Sermon into the basic ideas of the Big Book. The points were, of course, in the Sermon itself. In addition, the pioneers read many books and articles on and about the sermon which are thoroughly documented in my title, *The Good Book and The Big Book: A.A.'s Roots in the Bible*. Those items further illustrate some of the points made in the Sermon and that might have found their way into A.A.

The Lord's Prayer—Matthew 6:9-13

Oxford Group meetings closed with the Lord's Prayer in New York and in Akron. In early A.A., the alcoholics also closed meetings with the Lord's Prayer. Moreover, I have personally attended at least two thousand A.A. meetings, and almost every one has closed with the Lord's Prayer. At the 1990 International A.A. Conference in Seattle, which was a first for me, some 50,000 members of Alcoholics Anonymous joined in closing their meetings with the Lord's Prayer. The question here concerns what parts, if any, of the Lord's Prayer found their way into the Big Book, Twelve Steps, A.A. Slogans, and the A.A. fellowship; and we hasten to remind the reader that the prayer is *part of the Sermon on the Mount.*

Here are the verses of the Lord's Prayer (*King James Version*) as found in Matt. 6:9-13. Jesus instructed the Judeans, "After this manner therefore pray ye":

> Our Father which art in heaven, Hallowed be thy name.
> Thy kingdom come. Thy will be done in earth, as *it is* in heaven. Give us this day our daily bread.
> And forgive us our debts, as we forgive our debtors.
> And lead us not into temptation, but deliver us from evil: For thine is the kingdom, and the power, and the glory, for ever. Amen.

Dr. Bob studied specific commentaries on the Sermon by Oswald Chambers, Glenn Clark, Emmet Fox, and E. Stanley Jones. And these writers extracted a good many teachings, prayer guides, and theological ideas from Lord's Prayer verses in the Sermon. But there are a few concepts and phrases in the Lord's Prayer itself which either epitomize A.A. thinking or can be found in its language—whether or not the A.A. traces came from the Lord's Prayer or from other portions of the Bible. For example, the Big Book uses the word "Father" when referring to the Creator Yahweh, our God; and the context shows that this usage and name came from the Bible. The Oxford Group also used the term "Father," among other names, when referring to God. The concept and expression of God as "Father" is not confined to the Sermon on the Mount. It can be found in many other parts of the New Testament. But AAs have given the "Our Father" prayer a special place in their meetings. Thus the Lord's Prayer seems the likely source of their use of the word "Father."

The phrase "Thy will be done" is directly quoted, or is the specific subject of reference, in the Big Book several times (Big Book, 4th ed., pp. 63, 67, 76, 85, 88). It underlies A.A.'s oft-mentioned contrast between "self-will" and "God's will." The Oxford Group stressed, as do A.A.'s Third and Seventh Step prayers, that there must be a *decision to do God's will and surrender to His will.* These ideas were also symbolized in the A.A. prayer's "Thy will be done."

Finally, "Forgive us our "debts" or "trespasses" certainly states that God can and will "forgive;" and these concepts can be found in the Big Book, whether they came from the Lord's Prayer or from other important Biblical sources such as the Book of James (James 5:16), the writings of Paul in Colossians 3:13, and 1 John 1:9.

Our own discussion will review Jesus' Sermon, chapter by chapter. It will pinpoint some principal thoughts that Dr. Bob and Bill may have had in mind when they each said that the Sermon on the Mount contained the underlying philosophy of Alcoholics Anonymous. Here follows our review:

Matthew Chapter 5

***The Beatitudes*:** The Beatitudes are found in Matt. 5:3-11. The word "beatitudes" refers to the first word "Blessed" in each of these verses. Merriam Webster's says "blessed" means "enjoying the bliss of heaven." The word in the Greek New Testament from which "blessed" was translated means, "happy," according Biblical scholar Ethelbert Bullinger. *Vine's Expository Dictionary of Old and New Testament Words* explains the word "Blessed" as follows: "In the beatitudes the Lord indicates not only the characters that are blessed, but the nature of that which is the highest good." Dr. Bob's wife Anne Smith described the Beatitudes in the Sermon on the Mount as "the Christ-like virtues to be cultivated." Dick B., *Anne Smith's Journal,* p. 135.

The beatitude verses can be found at the very beginning of Jesus's sermon and read as follows:

> And seeing the multitudes, he went up into a mountain: and when he was set, his disciples came unto him:
> And he opened his mouth, and taught them, saying,
> Blessed are the poor in spirit: for theirs is the kingdom of heaven.
> Blessed are they that mourn: for they shall be comforted.
> Blessed are the meek: for they shall inherit the earth.
> Blessed are they which do hunger and thirst after righteousness: for they shall be filled.
> Blessed are the merciful: for they shall obtain mercy.

Blessed are the pure in heart: for they shall see God.
Blessed are the peacemakers: for they shall be called the children of God.
Blessed are they which are persecuted for righteousness' sake: for theirs is the kingdom of heaven.
Blessed are ye, when men shall revile you, and persecute you, and shall say all manner of evil against you falsely, for my sake.
Rejoice, and be exceeding glad: for great is your reward in heaven: for so persecuted they the prophets which were before you (Matt. 5:1-12)

Italicized below are *Webster's* definitions for the key words in each "beatitude" verse. Included also are quotes from the *King James Version*, which was the version Dr. Bob and early AAs most used. As the verses appear in the King James, they state: "Blessed" are:

- the poor *(humble)* in spirit [renouncing themselves, wrote E. Stanley Jones]: for theirs is the kingdom of heaven (v. 3);

- they that mourn *(feel or express grief or sorrow):* for they shall be comforted (v. 4);

- the meek *(enduring injury with patience and without resentment);* for they shall inherit the earth (v. 5);

- they which do hunger and thirst after righteousness *(acting in accord with divine or moral law):* for they shall be filled (v. 6);

- the merciful *(compassionate):* for they shall obtain mercy (v. 7);

- the pure *(spotless, stainless)* in heart [has a passion for righteousness and a compassion for men–seeks law and shows love, wrote Jones]: for they shall see God (v. 8);

- the peacemakers: for they shall be called the children of God (v. 9);

- they which are persecuted for righteousness sake: for theirs is the kingdom of heaven (v. 10);

- ye when men shall revile you, and persecute you, and shall say all manner of evil against you falsely, for my sake *(end or purpose):* for great is your reward in heaven: for so persecuted they the prophets which were before you (v. 11).

Did Dr. Bob, Anne, Bill, or Henrietta Seiberling study and draw specifically on these beatitude verses as they put together A.A.'s Akron recovery program? The author can neither provide nor document any answer. But there are some ideas common to A.A.'s spiritual principles in the beatitudes as you see them expressed above. These are:

(1) Humility–overcoming self;

(2) Comfort for the suffering;

(3) Patience and tolerance to the end of eliminating resentment;

(4) Harmonizing one's actions with God's will;

(5) Compassion, which *Webster* defines as "sympathetic consciousness of others distress together with a desire to alleviate;"

(6) "Cleaning house"–which means seeking obedience to God and, based on the principles of love, straightening out harms caused by disobedience;

(7) Making peace;

(8) Standing for and acting upon spiritual principles, whatever the cost, because they are God's principles.

The foregoing are Twelve Step ideas that can be found in the Beatitudes; and A.A. founders probably saw them there as well They can most certainly be found in the Big Book. Thus the Big Book frequently emphasizes humility, comforting others, patience and tolerance, "Thy will be done," compassion, amends, peacemaking, emulating these as "cardinal principles of Jesus Christ" which Anne Smith suggested were Christ-like virtues to be cultivated.

Letting your light shine: Matt. 5:13-16 suggest glorifying your Heavenly Father by letting others *see* your good works in practice. That is, "Letting your light shine" does not mean glorifying yourself, but rather glorifying God by letting others see your spiritual walk *in action*—see the immediate results of your surrender to the Master. These ideas may be reflected in the Big Book's statement: "Our real purpose is to fit ourselves to be of maximum service to God. . . ." (p. 77).

Obeying the Ten Commandments In Matt. 5:17-21, Jesus reiterates the importance of obeying the law and the prophets, specifically referring to Exod. 20:13 (Thou shalt not kill), but obviously referring as well to the other important commandments such as having no other god but Yahweh (Exod. 20:2-3), worshiping no other god (Exod. 20:4-5), eschewing adultery (Exod. 20:14), refraining from stealing (Exod. 20:15), and so on. And even though some of these commandments may have fallen between the cracks in today's A.A., they very clearly governed the moral standards of early A.A. that Dr. Bob and the Akron AAs embraced. The Ten Commandments were part of early A.A. pamphlets and literature, and (for example) Dr. Bob and the Akron AAs would have nothing to do with a man who was committing adultery (See *DR. BOB*, supra, p. 131 – Item Number 3).

The Law of Love in Action: In Matt. 5:17-47, Jesus confirms that the Law of Love fulfills the Old Testament Law. He rejects anger without cause, unresolved wrongs to a brother, quibbling with an adversary, lust and impurity, adultery, retaliation, and hatred of an enemy. The author's title *The Oxford Group & Alcoholics Anonymous* covers many of these ideas as roots of A.A. principles. And such materials in these verses in Matthew may very well have influenced A.A. language about:

*(a) **Overcoming Resentments***: Matthew 5:22:

> ". . . I say unto you, That whosoever is angry with his brother without a cause shall be in danger of the judgment. . ." *See Alcoholics Anonymous* 4th ed., p. 67: "God save me from being angry."

(b) *Making restitution*—Matthew 5:23-24:

> "Therefore if thou bring thy gift before the altar, and there rememberest that thy brother hath ought against thee; Leave there thy gift before the altar, and go thy way; first be reconciled to thy brother, and then come and offer thy gift;" See *DR. BOB*, p. 308: "We learned what was meant when Christ said, "Therefore if thou bring thy gift to the altar. . . "

(c) *Avoidance of retaliation for wrongdoing by others*—Matthew 5:38-39:

> 'Ye have heard that it hath been said, An eye for an eye, and a tooth for a tooth: But I say unto you, That ye resist not evil: but whosoever shall smite thee on thy right cheek, turn to him the other also;" See *Alcoholics Anonymous,* 4th ed., p. 67: "Though we did not like their symptoms and the way these disturbed us. . . . We avoid retaliation or argument. . . . at least God will show us how to take a kindly and tolerant view of each and every one."

(d) *Making peace with our enemies*—Matthew 5:43-44:

> "Ye have heard that it hath been said, Thou shalt love thy neighbor, and hate thine enemy. But I say unto you. Love your enemies, bless them that curse you, do good to them that hate you, and pray for them which despitefully use you, and persecute you." See *Alcoholics Anonymous*, 4th ed., pp. 67, 70: "When a person offended we said to ourselves, "This is a sick man. How can I be helpful to him? . . . Thy will be done. . . . We have begun to learn tolerance, patience, and good will

toward all men, even our enemies, for we look on them as sick people."

Matthew Chapter 6

Anonymity. Matt. 6:1-8, 16-18—urge almsgiving "in secret," praying "in secret," fasting "in secret," and avoiding "vain repetitions," and hypocrisy. These verses could very possibly have played a role in the development of A.A.'s spiritual principle of anonymity. Jesus said, "your Father knoweth what things ye have need of, before ye ask him" and "thy Father, which seeth in secret, shall reward thee openly." The vain practices which Jesus condemned were acts focusing on self-importance, inflating the ego, and manifesting self-centeredness--something A.A. disdains. Making a public display of gift-giving, praying, fasting, and repetitive prayers was something Jesus criticized because *of* the pointless hypocrisy of showing off one's feigned piety to men whereas the almsgiving, fasting, and prayers were really addressed to or for or in worship of God, Who already knew the heart of the hypocrite. *See Alcoholics Anonymous*, 4th ed., p. 62: "Selfishness—self-centeredness! That, we think, is the root of our troubles. . . . Above everything, we alcoholics must be rid of this selfishness." Early Oxford Group and A.A. literature often spoke of "God-sufficiency" versus "self-sufficiency," and "God-centeredness" versus "self-centeredness." We have located no direct tie between Jesus' teachings on anonymity and A.A.'s Traditions on this principle. But the concepts are parallel; and *The Runner's Bible,* and other A.A. biblical sources that AAs studied, do discuss their significance at some length. Also, see *Alcoholics Anonymous*, 4th ed., pp. 76, 77, 93:

> Our real purpose is to fit ourselves to be of maximum service to God and the people around us. . . . We will lose interest in selfish things and gain interest in our fellows. Self-seeking will slip away. . . . To be vital, faith must be accompanied by self-sacrifice and unselfish, constructive action.

Forgiveness. Matt. 6:14-15 refer to forgiving men their trespasses; and Emmet Fox's forceful writing about these verses exemplifies the A.A. amends process. Fox said:

> The forgiveness of sins is the central problem of life. . . . It is, of course, rooted in selfishness. . . . We must positively and definitely extend forgiveness to everyone to whom it is possible that we can owe forgiveness, namely, to anyone who we think can have injured us in any way. . . When you hold resentment against anyone, you are bound to that person by a cosmic link, a real, tough metal chain. You are tied by a cosmic tie to the thing that you hate. The one person perhaps in the whole world whom you most dislike is the very one to whom you are attaching yourself by a hook that is stronger than steel. Fox, *The Sermon on the Mount,* pp. 183-88.

There is no assurance that Fox's writing on the sermon's forgiveness point specifically influenced the Big Book's emphasis on forgiveness. To be sure, at least two A.A. history writers have claimed that Fox's writings did influence Bill Wilson. However, other books that were read by early AAs–books by such authors as Henry Drummond, Glenn Clark, E. Stanley Jones, and Harry Emerson Fosdick–used language similar to that used by Fox in his discussion of forgiveness of enemies. And Jesus' Sermon on the Mount is not the only place in the New Testament where forgiveness is stressed. Thus, after, and even though, Christ had accomplished remission of past sins of believers, Paul wrote:

> Forbearing one another, and forgiving one another, if any man have a quarrel against any: even as Christ forgave you, so also *do ye* (Col. 3:13)

See also the following verse, a favorite often quoted and used by Henrietta Seiberling–the well known early A.A. teacher who was often thought of as an A.A. founder:

> If a man say I love God, and hateth his brother. he is a liar: for he that loveth not his brother whom he hath seen, how can he love God whom he hath not seen? (1 John 4:20)

In any event, the Big Book, Fourth Edition, states at page 77:

> The question of how to approach the man we hated will arise. It may be he has done us more harm than we have done him

and, though we may have acquired a better attitude toward him, we are still not too keen about admitting our faults. Nevertheless, with a person we dislike, we take the bit in our teeth. It is harder to go to an enemy than to a friend, but we find it more beneficial to us. We go to him in a helpful *and forgiving spirit,* confessing our former ill feeling and expressing our regret. Under no condition do we criticize such a person or argue. Simply we tell him that we will never get over drinking until we have done our utmost to straighten out the past (italics added). [Note that Wilson makes no effort to argue for forgiveness because of Biblical authority]

"The sunlight of the Spirit?" Speaking of the futility and unhappiness in a life which includes deep resentment, the Big Book states: "when harboring such feelings we shut ourselves off from the sunlight of the Spirit." One often hears this "sunlight" expression quoted in A.A. meetings. Yet its origins seem unreported and undocumented. Anne Smith referred frequently in her journal to the verses in 1 John which had to do with fellowship with God and walking in the light as God is light. So did A.A.'s Oxford Group sources. And the following are the most frequently quoted verses from 1 John having to do with God as "light" and the importance of walking in the light (rather than walking in darkness) in order to have fellowship with Him:

> That which we have seen and heard declare we unto you, that ye may have fellowship with us: and truly our fellowship *is* with the Father, and with his Son, Jesus Christ.
> And these things write we unto you, that your joy may be full. This then is the message which we have heard of him, and declare unto you, that God is light, and in him is no darkness at all.
> If we say that we have fellowship with him, and walk in darkness, we lie, and do not the truth:
> But if we walk in the light, as he is in the light, we have fellowship one with another, and the blood of Jesus Christ his Son cleanseth us from all sin (1 John 1:3-7).

Though this particular discussion is concerned with the Sermon on the Mount, we have mentioned also the foregoing verses from 1 John 1:3-7 (having to do with walking in God's light as against opposed to walking in darkness). For very possibly those ideas in 1 John, together with the following verses in the Sermon, may have given rise to Bill's references to the alcoholic's being blocked from the "sunlight of the Spirit" when he or she dwells in such dark realms as fear and excessive anger. Matt. 6:22-24 (in the Sermon) state:

> The light of the body is the eye: if therefore thine eye be single, thy whole body shall be full of light.
> But if thine eye be evil, thy whole body shall be full of darkness. If therefore the light that is in thee be darkness, how great *is* that darkness!
> No man can serve two masters: for either he will hate the one, and love the other: or else he will hold to the one, and despise the other. Ye cannot serve God and mammon.

Seek ye first the kingdom of God. Matt. 6:24-34 seem to have had tremendous influence on A.A. At least on early A.A.! The substance of these verses is that man will be taken care of when he seeks *first* the kingdom of God and His righteousness. Verse 33 says:

> But seek ye first the kingdom of God, and his righteousness; and all these things [food. clothing, and shelter] shall be added unto you.

Dr. Bob specifically explained the origin of our A.A. slogans "Easy Does It" and "First Things First." *DR. BOB and the Good Oldtimers,* pp 135, 144, 192, 282. When he was asked the meaning of "First Things First," Dr. Bob replied. "Seek ye first the kingdom of God and His righteousness, and all these things shall be added unto you." He told his sponsee Clarence Snyder that "First Things First" came from Matt. 6:33 in the Sermon on the Mount. *DR. BOB*, p. 144. And this verse was widely quoted in the books that Dr. Bob and the Akron AAs read and recommended. Dick B., *The Good Book and The Big Book,* p. 125, n.119; *That Amazing Grace*, pp. 30, 38).

On page 60, the Big Book states the A.A. solution for relief from alcoholism: "God could and would if He were *sought*." (italics added).

This concept is one of "seeking" results by reliance on God instead of reliance on self. And this is a bedrock idea in the Big Book. *See Alcoholics Anonymous*, 4th ed., pp. 11, 14, 25, 28, 43, 52-53, 57, 62. In view of Dr. Bob's explanations as to the origin of "First Things First," the Big Book's emphasis on "seeking" very likely came from the "seeking the kingdom of God first" idea in Matt. 6:33.

According to Dr. Bob, the slogans "Easy Does It" and "One day at a time" came from the next verse–Matthew 6:34. See Dick B., *The Good Book and The Big Book*, pp. 87-88, and other citations therein. The Big Book glowingly endorses "three little mottoes" which are "First Things First; Live and Let Live; and Easy Does It" (*Alcoholics Anonymous*, 4th ed., p. 135). Two of the three very clearly have their roots in Matthew 6:24-34.

Matthew Chapter 7

Taking your own inventory. Much of A.A.'s Fourth, Ninth, Tenth, and Eleventh Step actions involve looking for your own part, for your own fault in troublesome matters. This self-examination process (as part of the house-cleaning and life-changing process in the Steps) was expected to result in that which, in Appendix II of the Fourth Edition of the Big Book, became described as "the personality change sufficient to bring about recovery from alcoholism" (Big Book, p. 567). Matt. 7:3-5 states:

> And why beholdest thou the mote [speck] that is in thy brother's eye, but considerest not the beam [log] that is in thine own eye?
> Or how wilt thou say to thy brother, Let me pull the mote [speck] out of thine eye; and, behold, a beam [log] *is* in thine own eye.
> Thou hypocrite, first cast out the beam [log] out of thine own eye; and then shalt thou see clearly to cast out the mote [speck] out of thy brother's eye.

These verses from Matthew were frequently cited by A.A.'s spiritual sources as the Biblical authority for self-examination and thus finding one's own part, one's own erroneous conduct, in a relationship problem. Anne Smith specifically wrote in her spiritual journal that she must look for the "mote" in her own eye. We've already discussed similar "inventory" ideas in James.

Ask, seek, knock. Matt. 7:7-11 states:

> Ask, and it shall be given you; seek, and ye shall find; knock, and it shall be opened unto you;
> For every one that asketh receiveth; and he that seeketh findeth; and to him that knocketh it shall be opened.
> Or what man is there of you, whom if his son ask bread, will he give him a stone? Or if he ask a fish, will he give him a serpent?
> If ye then, being evil, know how to give good gifts unto your children, how much more shall your Father which is in heaven give good things to them that ask him?

Bill Wilson's spiritual teacher, Rev. Sam Shoemaker—called by Bill a "co-founder of A.A."--wrote:

> Our part [in the crisis of self-surrender] is to ask, to seek, to knock. His [God's] part is to answer, to come, to open. Samuel M. Shoemaker, Jr. *Realizing Religion.* NY: Association Press, 1923, p. 32.

The Runner's Bible (one of the most important of the early A.A. Bible devotionals) has an entire chapter titled, "Ask and Ye shall receive." Another favored devotional among the A.A. pioneers was *My Utmost for His Highest,* by Oswald Chambers. Chambers says, about the foregoing verses beginning with Matt. 7:7:

> The illustration of prayer that Our Lord uses here is that of a good child asking for a good thing. . . . It is no use praying unless we are living as children of God. Then, Jesus says: "Everyone that asketh receiveth."

The foregoing verses, and relevant comments by A.A. sources, underline all the requisites in the asking and receiving concept. First, you must become a child of God. Then, establish a harmonious relationship with Him. And only *then* expect good results from the Creator, Yahweh, our God—expecting "Providence" from Him because He is in fact our Heavenly Father and cares about His childrens' needs.

Given the emphasis in early A.A. on the Sermon, those verses from Matt. 7 very probably influenced similar ideas expressed as follows in the Big Book's Fourth Edition:

> If what we have learned and felt and seen means anything at all, it means that all of us, whatever our race, creed, or color are the children of a living Creator with whom we may form a relationship upon simple and understandable terms as soon as we are willing and honest enough to try (p. 28).

> God will constantly disclose more to you and to us. Ask Him in your morning meditation what you can do each day for the man who is still sick. The answers will come, *if your own house is in order.* But obviously you cannot transmit something you haven't got. See *to it that your relationship with Him is right,* and great events will come to pass for you and countless others. This is the Great Fact for us (p. 164, italics added).

In this same vein. Dr. Bob's wife, Anne, wrote, in the spiritual journal she shared with early AAs and their families:

> We can't give away what we haven't got. We must have a genuine contact with God in our present experience. Not an experience of the past, but an experience in the present—actual, genuine. Dick B., *Anne Smith's Journal, 1933-1939. 3rd ed,* Kihei, HI: Paradise Research Publications, Inc., 1988, p. 121.

Do unto others. The so-called "Golden Rule" cannot, as such, be readily identified in A.A.'s Big Book though it certainly is a much-quoted portion of the Sermon on the Mount which Bill and Dr. Bob said underlies A.A.'s philosophy. The relevant verse is Matt. 7:12:

> Therefore all things whatsoever ye would that men should do to you, do ye even so to them: for this is the law and the prophets.

Perhaps the following two Big Book Fourth Edition segments bespeak that Golden Rule philosophy as Bill may have seen it:

> We have begun to learn tolerance, patience and good will toward all men, even our enemies, for we look on them as sick people. We have listed the people we have hurt by our conduct, and are willing to straighten out the past if we can (p. 70).

> Then you will know what it means to give of yourself that others may survive and rediscover life. You will learn the full meaning of "Love thy neighbor as thyself" (p. 153).

> In his last address to AAs, Dr. Bob said: "Our Twelve Steps, when simmered down to the last, resolve themselves into the words 'love' and 'service.' "(*DR. BOB*, pp. 77, 338).

I now know from my extensive research of the United Christian Endeavor Society, to which Dr. Bob belonged as a youngster in the North Congregational Church at St. Johnsbury, Vermont, that Christian Endeavor frequently spoke of "love and service;" and I have concluded that the original Akron fellowship's principles and practices seem very much patterned on those Dr. Bob embraced from his Christian Endeavor days. As one lead to what Dr. Bob might have taken from his early background on this point, note that Christian Endeavor's magazine was called the "Golden Rule"—which further highlights the significance of this "do unto others" concept in Dr. Bob's life and legacy. The frequent discussion by both Christian Endeavor and Dr. Bob of Biblical "love and service" can probably and appropriately be equated with the unselfish love and service implicit in the Sermon's "Golden Rule"—do unto others as you would have them do unto you.

He that doeth the will of my Father. There are *several* key verses in the Sermon on the Mount which could have caused Bob and Bill to say that Matthew Chapters Five to Seven contained A.A.'s underlying philosophy. The verses are in the Lords Prayer itself (Matt. 6:9-13), in the so-called Golden Rule quoted above (Matt. 7:12), and in the phrase "Thy will be done" (Matt. 6:10). Each or all could be considered among Dr. Bob's "fundamentals" and "essentials." In addition to these three sets of verses, however, I really believe that the major, the "fundamental," the "essential," and the "underlying" spiritual A.A. philosophy borrowed by the founders from the Sermon on the Mount—can be found in Matt. 7:21:

> Not every one that saith unto me. Lord, Lord, shall enter into the kingdom of heaven; but he that doeth the will of my Father which is in heaven.

Do the will of Yahweh our Creator, Who was the Father of Jesus. That is the injunction in these last verses of the Sermon. Bill Wilson said clearly in the Big Book and in his other writings that the key requirement in A.A. is doing the will of the Father-the Father Who is the *subject* of the Lord's Prayer; Almighty God –Whose will was to be done; the Creator upon whom early AAs relied as they sought to "find" and obey Him. Note that Wilson wrote:

> I was to sit quietly when in doubt, asking only for direction and strength to meet my problems as He would have me (Bill's Story, Big Book, 4th ed., p. 13).

> He humbly offered himself to his Maker—then he knew (Big Book, 4th ed., p. 57).

> . . . praying only for knowledge of His will for us and the power to carry that out (Step Eleven, Big Book, 4th ed., p. 59).

> May I do Thy will always (portion of "Third Step Prayer," Big Book, 4th ed., p. 63)!

> Thy will be done (Big Book, 4th ed, pp. 67, 88).

> Grant me strength, as I go out from here, to do your bidding. Amen (portion of "Seventh Step Prayer," Big Book, 4th ed., p. 76).

There is God, our Father, who very simply says, 'I am waiting for you to do my will.' *Alcoholics Anonymous Comes of Age,* p. 105.

From a long literary and religious heritage, the Oxford Group, Rev. Sam Shoemaker, and Bill Wilson acquired and expressed the simple idea that God has a plan, and that man's chief end is to accomplish that plan. See Frank Buchman, *Remaking the World,* pp. 48, 53, 63, 77, 78, 101, 144; A. J. Russell, *For Sinners Only,* p. 23; Samuel M. Shoemaker, *Children of the Second Birth,* p. 27; Dick B., *The Oxford Group and Alcoholics Anonymous,* pp. 158-160, 40-41; *New Light on Alcoholism,* p. xiii.

In his treatise, *The Ideal Life,* published in 1897, Professor Henry Drummond (also the author of *The Greatest Thing in the World*—to be discussed in a moment)—quoted the following from Acts, Chapter 23:

> And afterward they desired a king: and God gave unto them Saul. . . . And when he had removed him, he raised up unto them David to be their king: to whom also he gave testimony, and said, I have found David, the son of Jesse, a man after mine own heart, which shall fulfill all my will. Of this man's seed hath God according to his promise raised unto Israel a Saviour, Jesus (verses 21-23)

Drummond then set forth his basic theme of the "Ideal" life." It was devoted to David— "The Man After God's Own Heart: A Bible Study on the Ideal of a Christian Life." He took King David as his example because God said David was a man after His own heart—who "shall" fulfill my will. Eloquently, Drummond wrote, as part of his essays in the *The Ideal Life*:

> Now we are going to ask to-day, What is the true plan of the Christian life? We shall need a definition that we my know it, a description that we may follow it. And if you look, you will see that both, in a sense, lie on the surface of our text. "A man after Mine own heart,"—here is the definition of what we are to be. "Who shall fulfil all my Will."—here is the description of how we are to be it. These words are the definition and the description of the model human life. They describe the man

after God's own heart. They give us the key to the Ideal Life. The general truth of these words is simply this: that the end of life is to do God's will. Henry Drummond. *The Greatest Thing in the World.* London and Glasgow: Collins Clear-Type Press, n.d., p. 203.

Dr. Bob owned all the Drummond books. I saw them as I poured over his "library" consisting of about half the books in the attic of his daughter Sue Smith Windows. I saw Drummond books in the lists Sue and her brother Smitty wrote to me in their own hand and in the books Smitty donated to Dr. Bob's Home in Akron. Dr. Bob read them. His name and address were written in his own hand in most. And Sue even phoned me shortly before her death asking me to confirm for her my belief in the importance of Drummond's *Natural Law in the Spiritual World*—one of Dr. Bob's books which we had reviewed in her attic.

And what about Bill? Well, we know for sure that he at least *heard* all the Oxford Group ideas. We know he said that he and Dr. Bob felt O.G. ideas had "seeded" A.A. And Bill probably talked more about "Thy will be done" and doing God's will than any other Biblical concept he borrowed for the Big Book.

Now let's turn to a very basic question which should have been put directly to Bill Wilson and Dr. Bob: What, then, was the source of the underlying philosophy of A.A. in the Sermon?

I don't know!

Take your choice. It could have been the Lord's Prayer. It could have been "Thy will be done" in the Lord's Prayer. It could have been the Golden Rule—a probability at which Dr. Bob once hinted. It could have been the Beatitudes. It could have been "love thy neighbor, and even thine enemies." It could have been "First Things First:--"seek ye first the kingdom of God and His righteousness." But the most forceful of the Sermon's declarations seemed to be:

> Not everyone that saith unto me, Lord Lord, shall enter into the kingdom of heaven; but he that doeth the will of my Father which is in heaven (Matthew 7:22).

This fundamental is also expressed in the Old Testament in these words from Ecclesiastes 12:13:

> Let us hear the conclusion of the whole matter. Fear God, and keep his commandments: for this is the whole duty of man.

I like some of the following words about Bob and what Bill and others had to say about him:

> Prayer, of course, was an important part of Dr. Bob's faith. According to Paul S., "Dr. Bob's morning devotion consisted of a short prayer, a 20-minute study of a familiar verse from the Bible, and a quiet period of waiting for directions as to where he, that day, should find use for his talent. Having heard, he would religiously go about his Father's business, as he put it." *DR. BOB,* p. 314.

The Gospel of Luke tells us that, at age 12, Jesus "tarried behind in Jerusalem" after his parents had left. Three days later, they found him in the temple, sitting in the midst of the doctors, both hearing them, and asking them questions. They all were astonished at his understanding and answers. His parents saw him; chewed him out for tarrying; but were than to hear Jesus reply to them:

> How is it that ye sought me? Wist ye not that I must be about my Father's business? (See Luke 2:43-49)

In other words, don't you realize that "my Father's business" comes first. Doing His will comes first. Seek ye first His kingdom. Man's whole duty is to keep His commandments.

In its biography of Dr. Bob, A.A. reported that Dr. Bob, when he was conducting surgery and wasn't sure, would pray before he started, as to which Bob commented:

> "When I operated under those conditions, I never made a move that wasn't right". . . . Whenever he got stuck about something, he always prayed about it. . . . He prayed, not only for his own understanding, but for different groups of people who requested him to pray for them, said Bill Wilson . . .

"Bob was far ahead of me in that sort of activity." *DR. BOB*, pp. 314-15.

Opinions are not always held in high regard in today's A.A. But I'll have a shot at this one: I believe that endeavoring to do the will of the Creator—as it is set forth in the Bible or as God may reveal it to an individual—constitutes A.A.'s underlying philosophy as spelled out in the Sermon on the Mount, of which Bob and Bill spoke.

Our Study of 1 Corinthians 13

1 Corinthians 13 is often called the Bible's "love" chapter because it focuses on the importance of love in the Christian's life. In the *King James Version*, the word "charity" is used in the verses which are speaking of "love;" but the underlying Greek word is *agapē* which is more properly translated "love."

And the most frequently quoted characteristics of love are contained in the following verses from the *King James Version* of the Bible (which is the version the A.A. pioneers used):

> Charity [love] suffereth long, *and* is kind; charity envieth not; charity vaunteth not itself, is not puffed up,
> Doth not behave itself unseemly, seeketh not her own, is not easily provoked, thinketh no evil;
> Rejoiceth not in iniquity, but rejoiceth in the truth (1 Cor. 13:4-6).

The *New International Version*, which is much in use today, renders 1 Cor. 13:4-6:

> Love is patient, love is kind. It does not envy, it does not boast, it is not proud.
> It is not rude, it is not self-seeking, it is not easily angered, it keeps no record of wrongs.
> Love does not delight in evil but rejoices with the truth.

One of the most popular books in early A.A. was Professor Henry Drummond's study of 1 Corinthians 13. The title of his book, *The Greatest Thing in the World,* was taken from the last verse of 1 Corinthians chapter 13, which reads:

And now abideth faith, hope, charity, these three; but the greatest of these is charity (1 Cor. 13:13).

Drummond's book was part of Dr. Bob's library, and a copy was still found in, and owned by, Dr. Bob's family when the author interviewed Dr. Bob's son and daughter several years ago. In much earlier years, A.A. Old-timer Bob E. had sent a memo to Bill Wilson's wife, Lois, in which Bob E. listed *The Greatest Thing in the World* as one of three books Dr. Bob regularly provided to alcoholics with whom he worked. In fact, Dr. Bob's enthusiasm for Drummond's book is dramatized by the following remarks by a former wife of A.A. old-timer Clarence S. Clarence's former wife, Dorothy S. M., said:

> Once, when I was working on a woman in Cleveland, I called and asked him [Dr. Bob], "What do I do for somebody who is going into D.T.'s?" He told me to give her the medication, and he said, "When she comes out of it and she decides she wants to be a different woman, get her Drummond's 'The Greatest Thing in the World.' Tell her to read it through every day for 30 days, and she'll be a different woman." See *DR. BOB and the Good Oldtimers,* p. 310.

Henry Drummond himself had made a similar suggestion half a century earlier, at the close of the lecture in which he delivered his 'greatest thing in the world' address–the address which was later published in Drummond's best-seller. Drummond said:

> Now I have all but finished. How many of you will join me in reading this chapter [1 Corinthians 13] once a week for the next three months? A man did that once and it changed his whole life. Will you do it? It is for the greatest thing in the world. You might begin by reading it every day, especially the verses which describe the perfect character. "Love suffereth long, and is kind; loveth envieth not; love vaunteth not itself." Get these ingredients into your life. See Drummond, *The Greatest Thing in the World.* p. 53.

The important influence on A.A. that came from 1 Corinthians 13 can be seen in Drummond's own simplified description of love's *ingredients*. Drummond listed nine ingredients of "love" as he saw love specifically defined in that portion of that chapter of the Bible (See Drummond, *The Greatest Thing in the World*, pp. 26-27). And we here set out those nine love ingredients with references to correlative Bible verses and correlative A.A. language:

Drummond's Explanation	Authorized KJV	NIV Version	A.A. Big Book 4th ed. Examples
1. Patience	"Charity suffereth long."	"Love is patient"	pp. 67, 70, 83, 111, 163
2. Kindness	"*and* is kind."	"love is kind"	pp. 67, 82, 83, 86
3. Generosity	"charity envieth not."	"It does not envy"	pp. 145, *cf.* 82
4. Humility	"charity vaunteth not itself"	"it does not boast"	pp. 13, 57, 68, 87-88
	"is not puffed up."	"it is not proud"	
5. Courtesy	"Doth not behave itself unseemly"	"It is not rude"	p. 69
6. Unselfishness	"seeketh not her own."	"It is not self-seeking"	pp. xxv, 93, 127
7. Good Temper	"is not easily provoked"	"it is not easily angered"	pp. 19, 67, 70, 83-84, 125, 118
8. Thinks no evil	"Rejoiceth not in iniquity"	it keeps no record of wrongs"	pp. 19, 67, 70, 83-84, 118, 125
	"Rejoiceth not in iniquity"	"does not delight in evil"	pp. xiv, xxvii, 13, 26, 28, 32, 44
9. Sincerity	"but rejoiceth in the truth"	"but rejoices with the truth"	pp. 47, 55, 57-58, 63-65, 67, 70, 73, 117, 140, 145

Dr. Bob said that A.A.'s Twelve Steps, when simmered down to the last, quite simply resolved themselves into the words "love" and "service." See *DR. BOB and the Good Oldtimers*, p. 338. He presented God to the old-timers as a God of love who was interested in their individual lives. *DR. BOB,* p. 110. Dr. Bob's wife, Anne, frequently quoted love verses in 1 John 4:8; 4:16–"God is love." *DR. BOB*, pp. 116-17. Furthermore both Anne and her husband Dr. Bob studied Toyohiko Kagawa's book, *Love: The Law of Life.* In that book, the author Kagawa devoted an entire chapter to 1 Corinthians 13, not only to the Corinthians chapter, but also to Drummond's analysis of that chapter in Drummond's *The Greatest Thing in the World*. Hence there was much emphasis among the A.A. pioneers on the "spiritual" principle of love as it is defined in the Bible. In fact, the Big Book itself talks repeatedly of that principle of love (Big Book, 4th ed., pp. 83-84, 86, 118, 122, 153).

Love, then--the love of God--was a much cherished principle in early A.A. The AAs needed it, wanted it, studied it, and sought to know it. Despite "higher power" divergences in current A.A. writings and meeting talk, the love of God is still a vital component of A.A.

thinking and speech. Even Bill Wilson inserted the phrase "a loving God" in A.A.'s Traditions. And I well remember my good friend Seymour W., a Jew, who tried each morning to comfort his many friends in the fellowship. The telephone on Seymour's "God" line would ring for many about 6:00 A.M. The message to the bedraggled A.A. was "God loves you." And Seymour would hang up. It was a coveted privilege to be on Seymour's "God-loves-you" list. What a way to start the day in early sobriety!

Further illustrating the great store placed on God's love and on the Corinthians love principle by A.A. pioneers is their frequent rendition of Jesus Christ's message in Mark 12:30-31. These Gospel verses deal with what Jesus called the two *great* commandments:

> And thou shalt love the Lord thy God with all thy heart, and with all thy soul, and with all thy mind, and with all thy strength; this is the first commandment. And the second is like, namely this, Thou shalt love thy neighbor as thyself. There is none other commandment greater than these.

The foregoing verses, from the Gospel of Mark in the New Testament, were cited for the standard of "Absolute Love," as it was discussed in AA of Akron's *A Manual for Alcoholics Anonymous* (one of the four pamphlets commissioned by Dr. Bob for use among early AAs). The Old Testament also contained the very same commandments to which Jesus referred, underlining the importance of love of God and of neighbor in all the commandments of the Bible:

> Hear, O Israel: The Lord our God *is* one Lord: And thou shalt love the Lord thy God with all thine heart, and with all thy soul, and with all thy might (Deut. 6:4-5).

> Thou shalt not avenge, nor bear any grudge against the children of thy people, but thou shalt love thy neighbor as thyself: I *am* the Lord (Lev. 19:18).

A.A. literature contains no specifics on, or detailing of, the impact of, 1 Corinthians 13 on A.A. But this cherished "essential," as Dr. Bob put it, deserves to be revived, promulgated, and applied today. The particulars can be seen by reading 1 Corinthians 13 itself; by noting the frequent mention of "Love" in the Big Book; by studying the reading and remarks of Dr. Bob and Anne; by remembering Bill Wilson's specific mention of Corinthians; and by the repeated mention of 1 Corinthians 13 in A.A.'s religious sources. The nine love "ingredients," as they were summarized by Henry Drummond, permeate A.A.'s basic text and can fairly be proclaimed to be among those "principles to be practiced" at the level of A.A.'s Twelfth Step. Regrettably, Wilson just plain ignored all the "principles" in his Twelfth Step chapter.

The fundamental principle is, of course, love. The component "ingredients" or "virtues" involved in such love are: patience; tolerance; kindness; humility; honesty; unselfishness; consideration for others; and the avoidance of anger, jealousy, envy, pride, and wrongdoing.

As previously covered, almost every one of these virtues can be found as well in Jesus' sermon on the mount and in the Book of James. The principles are defined in the sermon on the mount in specific terms that elaborate upon what constitutes doing the will of God in the love category. And, in James, from the standpoint of action and service to God and service to others through reliance upon God.

These were also the very the principles of love and service of which Dr. Bob spoke in his farewell address and defined as the essence of A.A.'s spiritual program of recovery.

Part 3: The Substantial Changes in A.A. from 1939 to 1955

The Original Big Book Thinking: The Akron Program and the Success Stories

Bill Wilson came to Akron in 1938—when the success of that program had been confirmed and acclaimed. He wanted authorization from the fellowship to write a book, open hospitals, and field missionaries. After a heated controversy, and by a vote margin of only two votes, Wilson secured his approval. And it appeared clear that Wilson was to write a basic text describing the program, and that personal stories of the pioneers were to be included as testimony of its success.

But that is not what happened at all.

The Wilson-Parkhurst Business Venture

Bill returned to New York. He and his business partner Hank Parkhurst, an alcoholic, formed a publishing corporation. The duly incorporated business was called "Works Publishing Company;" and stock shares were issued with intent to sell them primarily to alcoholics. A prospectus explained the stock offering. An outline of the proposed new book was drafted by Hank Parkhurst. But none of this in any way resembled the program of Akron.

What really happened instead was that Bill focused on his own story—first placing it as a second chapter of the new book and then moving it into first position, as the famous "Bill's Story." Included in that story and in the later portions of the basic text were all the elements of a modified Oxford Group program by which Bill began his quest for sobriety—coupling in its language a host of stories and resources which made up the "New York Genesis of A.A." At one point, Bill wanted to name the book after himself. Then it was understood that the book was to be called "The James Club." But upon final presentation, the name *Alcoholics Anonymous* was adopted.

Bill coined descriptions of an intermediate outline of the supposed program being used in Akron and elsewhere. He called them "word of mouth" ideas—despite the fact that Frank Amos had plainly outlined the elements of the actual, original program in Akron

Diversions from Akron's Program Called the Word-of-Mouth "Six Steps"

Set forth above are the seven points of the original A.A. program, as Frank Amos summarized them after careful investigation. Set forth too are quite detailed descriptions of exactly how AAs conducted their program—in terms of structure, hospitalization, work with newcomers, Bible study, prayer, reading of literature, utilization of some Oxford Group ideas, utilization of devotionals, utilization of Anne Smith's Journal, utilization of the Four Absolutes, confession of Christ, reliance on the Creator, obedience to God's will, and cleansing sin from one's conduct.

Dr. Bob said several times that he didn't write the 12 Steps and had nothing to do with writing them. He said their basic ideas came from A.A.'s study of and effort in the Bible. He said the Book of James, Jesus's Sermon on the Mount, and 1 Corinthians 13 were absolutely essential to the program.. And he specifically said that, when A.A. began, there were no Steps; there were no traditions; and that the stories (drunkalogs) didn't amount to much. So far, then, we've provided an almost complete composite of what early AAs did, developed, and accomplished from their founding on June 10, 1935 through the publication of their Big Book in the Spring of 1939.

But there were curious sideshows—call them "diversions"—that seemed to accompany or follow the first years of the Akron program. Bill Wilson began claiming there were six "word of mouth" elements being used for recovery. Yet there is no mention of them by Frank Amos or by Dr. Bob. Secondly, as Bill went in to a deep depression in the 1940's and 1950's, Dr. Bob seemed concerned about confusion as to the principles and practices of early A.A.—principles and practices that were to have been made the subject of the original basic text. Dr. Bob took pains to present the Akron program in writing in very simple form. And so it was that four Akron AA pamphlets emerged; and the pamphlets far more resembled the Frank Amos program than Bill's "six" word-of-mouth ideas or the elements of the Twelve Steps he wrote in the Big Book.

For a long time in my research, I kept hearing that there had been six steps before there were Twelve. In one way or another, Bill Wilson suggested this. In another way, Lois Wilson suggested it by quoting "six" Oxford Group tenets—tenets which very clearly did not exist in the history or annals of the Oxford Group. My tendency, therefore, was to point to these facts and reject Bill's "six" steps as bogus.

But I nonetheless encountered them in several different ways, phrased in several different forms, and emanating from several different alleged sources. The first phraseology appeared on a piece of paper handed to me in New York by Bill's secretary, Nell Wing. It was scribbled in Bill's handwriting; and it appeared to contain material identical to that which Bill had placed in an A.A. Grapevine article. Bill stated there, as "we commenced to form a Society separate from the Oxford Group, we began to state our principles something like this:

> We admitted we were powerless over alcohol.
> We got honest with ourselves.
> We got honest with another person, in confidence.
> We made amends for harms done others.
> We worked with other alcoholics without demand for prestige or money.
> We prayed to God to help us do these things as best we could"

See Dick B., *The Akron Genesis of Alcoholics Anonymous*, 3rd ed., 1998, pp. 256-257. Identical language—specifying **"we prayed to God"** can be found elsewhere. Not "a" god. Not God as you understand Him. Not whatever kind of God you thought there was. See Bill W., *The Language of the Heart*. NY: The AA Grapevine, Inc. 1988, p. 200; William L. White, *Slaying the Dragon*. IL: Chestnut Health Systems, 1998, p. 132.

Time marched on. Bill shifted gears, seemingly bent on putting still more distance between "God," the Akron program about God, and Bill's delegated responsibility to report the original facts in the new text he proposed. And Bill still talked about a "word-of-mouth" program of six steps to achieve and maintain sobriety. But Bill listed a new and rephrased "six steps" as follows; and the dutiful revisionist historians of A.A. followed suit:

> We admitted that we were licked, that we were powerless over alcohol.
> We made a moral inventory of our defects or sins.
> We confessed or shared our shortcomings with another person in confidence.
> We made restitution to all those we had harmed by our drinking.
> We tried to help other alcoholics, with no thought of reward in money or prestige.
> We prayed to whatever God we thought there was for power to practice these precepts.

See Dick B., *The Akron Genesis*, p. 256; *Alcoholics Anonymous Comes of Age*, p. 160*: Pass It On.*, p. 197; Ernest Kurtz, *Not-God*. MN: Hazelden, 1991, p. 69. Note the prayer to "**whatever God we thought there was**").

The newly invented six steps were not left alone, however. Others were tinkering with them. This even though there was absolutely no evidence that the Oxford Group had any steps at all – not two, nor four, nor six, nor twelve. But Bill's wife Lois declared that there were "the Oxford Group precepts"—six in number—as follows:

> Surrender your life to God.
> Take a moral inventory.
> Confess your sins to God and another human being.
> Make restitution.
> Give of yourself to others with no demand for return.
> Pray to God for help to carry out these principles.

See Dick B., *The Akron Genesis*, p. 257; *Lois Remembers*. NY: Al-Anon Family Group Headquarters, 1987, p. 92. Note the language **"surrender to God"** and **"Pray to God"**.

And then, after Dr. Bob was dead, came the following unsupported insertion in the Big Book. It alleged that Dr. Bob had used "six steps."

In language hardly resembling any ever used by Dr. Bob (who had also said *there were no steps*), the Big Book writer attributed the following words to Bob (words containing no mention of God):

> Complete deflation.
> Dependence and guidance from a Higher Power.
> Moral inventory.
> Confession.
> Restitution.
> Continued to work with alcoholics.

See Dick B., *The Akron Genesis*, p. 258; *Alcoholics Anonymous*, 2d ed., p. 292; *Alcoholics Anonymous Comes of Age*, pp. 22-23; *DR. BOB and the Good Oldtimers*, p. 131.

The Further Detours from Akron Program Ideas in the Words of Bill's New Twelve Steps

This is not a Twelve Step or a Big Book study. My title *Twelve Steps for You* covers the diverse origins of each of the Twelve Steps, examining each, step by step. The Big Book has been extensively studied and well reviewed by such venerable AAs as Joe McQ and Charlie P. in their Seminars, tapes, and books. What's been missing is an understanding of the fact that Bill Wilson was commissioned to write a basic text conveying the program details that were so successful in Akron by 1938. Instead, Wilson and his partner Hank Parkhurst, formed a corporation, drew up a stock prospectus, outlined a completely new and different recovery procedure, and sold the ultimate product as "the steps we took." This despite the fact that there were no steps, that the predecessor Oxford Group had no steps, and that no steps were ever taken by anyone in early 1939—the date the Big Book was published.

As a starting point, we can look at Bill's six word-of-mouth steps and the variant presentations of them. But it is important to highlight the things in the ultimate draft of Twelve Steps that completely changed A.A.'s ideas on what it took to recover. The draft threw Dr. Jung's "conversion" into a barrel and reworded it a "spiritual experience." Here are the highlights. See *Pass It On*, pp, 198-199:

- The idea that AAs were somehow "powerless" replaced the original concept that they were simply "licked." Powerless led more neatly to Bill's search for a "Power" Being licked had been a prelude to a cry to God for help out of the mire.
- The idea that AAs "came to believe" replaced the original concept that they either believed or they didn't. And "Power greater than themselves" replaced the word "God" to appease two or three atheists and fit the step into Bill's "Power" progression.
- The Third Step redefined "sin," characterized it as "self-centeredness," and put a spin on the surrender as being a surrender of self instead of a surrender to God—the kind of surrender involved in a real conversion.
- The Fourth through Seventh Steps involved action to eliminate offensive manifestations of self, rather than adopting the Biblical solution of receiving the spirit of God, walking by the Spirit, and disdaining walk by the flesh. Note the significance of this change in terms of the "cure" concept. "Self" can't be eliminated; hence never "cured." Walking in obedience to God's will is always possible and an attainable condition to cure.
- The restitution aspects of the Eighth and Ninth steps retained the Biblical ideas of agreeing with our adversary quickly, righting wrongs through restoration or reconciliation, and cleansing hands as suggested in James 4:7-10.
- The Tenth and Eleventh Steps shifted attention from a daily walk with the Creator to a daily effort to eliminate self-centeredness plus newly minted defects of character—resentment, self-seeking, dishonesty, and fear. They ignored the Four Absolute standards of Jesus that were so important to AAs and used in Akron—unselfishness, purity, honesty, love.
- The Twelfth Step twisted "conversion" to "spiritual experience" which offered no way to a new man in Christ, a new power of the Holy Spirit, and a new relationship with God. Quite frankly, no more dramatic shift in emphasis from God to self can be found elsewhere in the action steps. The Twelfth Step emphasized an experience

allegedly produced by action instead of a new creature, in Christ, produced by the Creator in the miracle a new birth. Its message therefore shifted to some undefined experience resulting from the steps taken, rather than a demonstration of what God does for man that man cannot do for himself. It spoke of principles but simply left them unspecified even though, in early A.A., the principles were taken from the Ten Commandments, the Sermon on the Mount, the Book of James, and 1 Corinthians 13, and other parts of the Bible.

The Whole Picture of the Diverse Sources that Influenced A.A.

Number One: The United Christian Endeavor Society. Organized in 1881, about the time of Dr. Bob's birth. Focused on the young people in a local Protestant Church which was supported by the Christian Endeavor Group connected with that church. The young people, including those in the Society to which Dr. Bob belonged at the North Congregational Church in St. Johnsbury, Vermont, were practicing almost all the major ideas that were carried over into early Akron A.A.'s Christian Fellowship led by Dr. Bob. The ideas? Confession of Christ. Bible study. Prayer meetings. Conversion meetings. Quiet Hours, topical discussions, reading of religious literature, witness, and fellowship—all under the banner of "love and service." Christian Endeavor's membership was world-wide and exceeded 3,500,000

Number Two: The Salvation Army. Organized under General William Booth not long after Christian Endeavor and plunged into helping homeless, outcasts, drunks, and street criminals. Their unselfish service work proved the success of abstinence, resisting temptation. confessing Jesus Christ as Saviour, relying on the Creator for guidance and strength, eliminating sin. Then effectively employing the power of one saved and recovered outcast to bring home to another still-suffering the message of salvation, love, and service. Also perpetuating fellowship and witness among those already saved, recovered soldiers. Weighing both the strengths and limitations of the Salvation Army with its 10,000 centers, various kinds of ministries carried on by 5,200 officers and 32,000 workers, the Rev. Dr. Howard Clinebell believes that the Army represents evangelistic therapy at its best and that some facilities have remarkable success in getting and keeping countless former homeless, low-bottom addicts sober and living constructive lives. Howard Clinebell. *Understandng and Counseling Persons with Alcohol, Drug, and Behavioral Addictions*. Nashville: Abingdon Press, 1998, pp. 157, 159. See also Dick B., *When Early AAs Were Cured and Why; The First Nationwide A.A. History Conference; A New Way Out.*

Number Three: Rescue and Gospel Missions. There are hundreds of missions today, and there were many in early A.A. days—providing "soup, soap, and salvation" to thousands upon thousands of down-trodden homeless and inebriate people. Both Bill Wilson and his sponsor Ebby Thacher went to Calvary Church's Rescue Mission; and both were aware of the evangelistic activities involving Bible teaching, prayer, hymns, and altar calls where Jesus Christ was accepted as Saviour. Though the records have been buried today, it is clear that many of the original New York A.A. manuscript materials contained "dogma and doctrines" from the mission programs. All were used and mentioned in the activities in Akron and even in New York. See Dick B. *A New Way Out, The Conversion of Bill W.*

Number Four: The conversion ideas of Dr. Carl Gustav Jung. Two or three historians who have not really done their homework now claim that Jung had no connection with A.A.'s beginnings. They assert that Jung never saw Rowland Hazard as a patient and therefore the "conversion" solution so dominant in Bill Wilson's Big Book program did not come from Jung. But such skimpy research has now been superseded. Moreover, it never did support the absurd conclusion that Jung, Rowland Hazard, Ebby Thacher, Bill Wilson, and Sam Shoemaker all lied in order to conjure up a solution. The real problem concerns how badly Wilson missed the point of Jung's idea of conversion. Conversion, Jung said, was the solution for Rowland's chronic alcoholism. But conversion, to Jung, did not mean what the Bible describes as a new birth and which Shoemaker and the Akronites were later espousing. Nor was Bill Wilson's response to the altar call at Shoemaker's Calvary Mission a conversion of the kind Jung had in mind. Nonetheless "conversion" became the foundational solution Wilson proposed for alcoholism, and Jung was called by Bill a "founder" of A.A.

Number Five: Professor William James and the "spiritual experience." Just who is the author of Bill's "spiritual experience" expression is not all that clear. Carl Jung told Rowland Hazard that Rowland needed a "conversion" experience. William James wrote *Varieties of Religious Experience*, which Wilson believed validated his "hot flash" experience—possibly a "spiritual experience"—at Towns Hospital. Finally, as he looked back on his life, Bill Wilson concluded he had had five spiritual experiences—possibly six if you accept his statement that his confessions to Father Dowling amounted to another "conversion experience." These experiences are covered in my forthcoming title, *The Conversion of Bill W.* Reverend Sam Shoemaker wrote in his first book *Realizing Religion* that people needed a "vital religious experience." Oxford Group writings are surfeited with references to "spiritual experience" and "spiritual awakening." So are Shoemaker's later books. Wilson liked to attribute the spiritual experience idea to James, an experience following "deflation-at-depth." Wilson also dubbed James a "founder" of A.A. And I certainly can and did find the James ideas Wilson mentioned and underlined the material in my titles *Turning Point: A History of Early A.A.'s Spiritual Roots and Successes* and *The Conversion of Bill W.*

Number Six: The role of Dr. Silkworth as a "founder" of A.A. has assumed new and far greater importance of late because of recent research into Silkworth's views about the cure of alcoholism by Jesus Christ and conversations he had with Wilson to that effect. There were also the medical ideas of Dr. William D. Silkworth. Once again, historians who have not really done their homework, sometimes claim that Dr. Silkworth did not originate the concept of alcoholism as a disease. To be sure, the disease concept itself has been challenged, and it may well not have originated with Silkworth. But there is equally strong evidence that it was Silkworth who spelled out for Bill Wilson the idea that Wilson was suffering from a mental obsession and a physical allergy—however the details were or would be characterized in a disease debate. Virtually unmentioned by historians, however, is Silkworth's belief—explained to Bill Wilson and other patients—that Jesus Christ, the "Great Physician," could cure them of alcoholism. Dick B. *The Good Book-Big Book Guidebook, The Conversion of Bill W.;* Peale, *The Positive Power of Jesus Christ;* Mitchel. *Silkworth—The Little Doctor Who Loved Drunks.*

Number Seven: The Oxford Group—A First Century Christian Fellowship. Not really "organized" until about 1919 when the book *Soul Surgery* was first published. Primarily a movement which drew its life-changing ideas from Biblical concepts of Lutheran Minister Frank N. D. Buchman. Each one of the aforementioned examples influenced various ideas that were borrowed and adapted by the Akron program. And to these were added catch-words and ideas that Buchman picked up during his group's actual founding. There were **twenty-eight ideas** in all that impacted upon A.A.'s Big Book and Twelve Steps and existed in greater or lesser degree in some of the practices in the earlier Akron Fellowship. The 28 ideas can be summarized in **eight groupings**: (1) **God**—descriptions of Him, His plan, man's duty, believing. (2) **Sin**—that which blocks us from God and others. (3) **Surrender**—the decision to surrender self and self-will to God's will. (4) **Life-changing art**—the Five C's process moving from Confidence to Confession to Conviction to Conversion to Continuance. (5) **Jesus Christ**—His power and the Four Absolute Standards. Buchman said: Sin was the problem. Jesus Christ was the cure. And the result was a miracle. (6) **Growth in fellowship** through Quiet Time, Bible study, prayer, and seeking Guidance. (7) **Restitution—for the harms caused by sin.** (8) **Fellowship and witness**—working in teams loyal to Jesus Christ to change the lives of others. Though Wilson was inclined for years to minimize and side-step the Oxford Group influence on the Big Book and Twelve Steps, the facts show otherwise. The Oxford Group ideas constitute the entire action part of Bill's step program. See Dick B. *The Oxford Group and Alcoholics Anonymous: A Design for Living That Works; The Akron Genesis of Alcoholics Anonymous; Turning Point: A History of the Spiritual Roots and Successes of Alcoholics Anonymous; A New Way Out; Twelve Steps for You.*

Number Eight: The teachings of Episcopalian priest Rev. Samuel M. Shoemaker, Jr. Sam teamed up with Frank Buchman about 1919 and then began writing an incredibly large series of books on OG ideas and Sam's Bible concepts. Sam headquartered his efforts at Calvary Church in New York, of which he became Rector in 1925. It is fair to say that the most quoted, the most copied, and the most persuasive influence on Bill Wilson and his Big Book approach came directly from Shoemaker. So said Bill himself. To the point where Wilson actually asked Sam to write the Twelve Steps, as to which Sam declined in favor of their being written by an alcoholic, namely, Bill. See Dick B. *New Light on Alcoholism: God, Sam Shoemaker, and A.A.; The First Nationwide History Conference; When Early AAs Were Cured and Why; By the Power of God; Twelve Steps for You.*

Number Nine: The lay therapy ideas of Richard Peabody. Dr. Bob and Bill Wilson both owned and studied *The Common Sense of Drinking*—a book by lay therapist Richard Peabody. And though Peabody died drunk, Wilson somehow saw fit to adopt almost verbatim certain words and phrases from the Peabody book. Among the two most unfortunate derivatives were: (1) There is no cure for alcoholism. (2) Once an alcoholic always an alcoholic. Both concepts flew in the face of a decade of clear and outspoken declarations by the early AAs and their observers that they had found a cure for alcoholism that rested on the power of Jesus Christ. Peabody simply didn't embrace Christianity as part of his therapy. And how Wilson got switched from God to incurable illness on the basis of the writings of a lay therapist who died drunk is currently a mystery to me. See Richard Peabody. *The Common Sense of Drinking;* Dick B. *Cured: Proven Help for Alcoholics and Addicts; When Early AAs Were Cured and Why; A New Way Out.*

Number Ten: The Biblical Emphasis from Dr. Bob's youth and Christian Endeavor contrasted with the New York influence from Sam Shoemaker. A.A. detractors and doctrinaire Christians who dislike the Oxford Group seem impelled to claim that A.A. came from the Oxford Group, that the Oxford Group was an heretical cult, and that its very existence was an example of what A.A. wasn't, rather than what it was. And these canards are so heavily entrenched in A.A. religious and recovery thinking and writing they may never be dispelled. But they are fallacious and utterly misleading. If you are a student of Oxford Group writings, you simply can't escape the obvious: Bill Wilson's Big Book and Twelve Step program embraced almost every Oxford Group idea—even though Bill Wilson used several ruses which were meant to deny the fact. By contrast, the early Akron program, which produced the 75 to 93% success rates, really had very little to do with Oxford Group missions, principles, and practices. The Akron focus was on abstinence—not an Oxford Group idea; hospitalization—not an Oxford Group idea; resisting temptation—not an Oxford Group idea; accepting Jesus Christ as Lord and Saviour—not an Oxford Group requirement; relying on the Creator for strength and guidance—a universal idea undoubtedly embraced by the Oxford Group; Bible study meetings—not an Oxford Group emphasis; old-fashioned prayer meetings—not an Oxford Group idea; Quiet Time—a universal idea which pre-dated the Oxford Group and was a big item in Christian Endeavor, the YMCA, and the Oxford Group; religious comradeship—not an Oxford Group idea; favored church attendance—not an Oxford Group idea; love and service as a banner—not an Oxford Group expression, and clearly Christian Endeavor words of art; working with others—not an Oxford Group emphasis when it came to alcoholism, nor was it particularly a Christian Endeavor idea except as to witnessing and conversion. By contrast, the simple Christian Endeavor program appears to represent the heart of what Akron did and what it was reported in official A.A. literature to have done. That program was not incorporated in the Big Book, but it is reported fully by Frank Amos reports to John D. Rockefeller, Jr. that are part of A.A.'s conference approved literature. See my titles Dick B. *The First Nationwide A.A. History Conference; The Good Book and The Big Book: A.A.'s Roots in the Bible; Why Early A.A. Succeeded (A Bible study primer); The Good Book-Big Book Guidebook*; *The James Club and The Early A.A. Program's Absolute Essentials; A New Way Out; Twelve Steps for You..*

Number Eleven: *The practical records and teachings of Dr. Bob's Wife.* How A.A. could have buried Anne Smith's role, her importance, and her spiritual journal is a complete mystery. The facts about Anne's importance would stand on their own even if she had never written her journal which spanned nine of A.A.'s formative years. As far as I've been able to discover, Bill never ever mentioned Anne's journal. Yet Bill Wilson and many pioneers called Anne the "Mother of A.A." The pioneer AAs were housed in her home from the beginning, and those AAs got well. AAs were fed in her home, and it became the first real "half-way" house after hospitalization. Anne read the Bible to A.A.'s founders and to the many who followed them. Anne conducted a quiet time each morning at the Dr. Bob's Home where she led a group of AAs and their families in Bible study, prayer, listening, and topical discussions. Anne counseled and nursed and taught alcoholics; and her work with newcomers in meetings was legendary. They were her special focus. Her journal records every principle and concept that is part of the A.A. picture—Bible studies, prayer, Quiet Time, Guidance, Literature recommended, Oxford Group principles and practices, and practical guides to working with alcoholics. It seems likely that she not only shared the contents of this journal—written between 1933 and 1939—with Bill Wilson, but also that Bill took many of his Oxford Group and other expressions directly from Anne's Journal. If so, the fact has never been mentioned. It's fair to say that Anne Smith—if she ever becomes the subject of proper research, recognition, and approbation—will be seen as a real bridge between the Biblical Christian Fellowship program of Akron and the Oxford Group/Shoemaker ideas that were embodied in Wilson's Steps and Big Book. Anne saw and discussed both. See Dick B. *Anne Smith's Journal, 1933-1939; The Akron Genesis of Alcoholics Anonymous; A New Way Out; Twelve Steps for You.*

Number Twelve: The Devotionals and Christian Literature Read and Circulated. We know that A.A.'s basic ideas came from the Bible. The Book of James, Jesus's Sermon on the Mount, and 1 Corinthians 13 were frequently read aloud and studied and were considered absolutely essential. And AAs studied literature that discussed these roots—books on the Sermon by Oswald Chambers, Glenn Clark, Harry Emerson Fosdick, Emmet Fox, and E. Stanley Jones. Devotionals discussing concepts from the Book of James—*The Runner's Bible, The Upper Room, My Utmost for His Highest, Daily Strength for Daily Needs.* There were commentaries on 1 Corinthians 13 written by Henry Drummond and Toyohiko Kagawa and studied by pioneers. And various other concepts were fleshed out through the literature of Shoemaker on all aspects of the Bible, prayer, guidance, Quiet Time, and so on. So also through the many Oxford Group books on these subjects—*Soul Surgery* (and the Five C's), *Quiet Time, The Guidance of God, Realizing Religion, For Sinners Only, When Man Listens*, and so on. In addition, there were prayer guides, Bible study guides, and healing guides galore—in Dr. Bob's Library and circulated by him to others. The whole picture can be found in my titles: Dick B. *The Books Early AAs Read for Spiritual Growth, 7th edition; Making Known the Biblical History and Roots of A.A.; Anne Smith's Journal; The Akron Genesis of Alcoholics Anonymous; Dr. Bob and His Library.*

Number Thirteen: New Thought. Also beginning to take wing through the impetus of Christian Science and similar movements that flowered at almost the same period as the first two examples. But the New Thought focus was on a new kind of god—a higher power—that took descriptive words from the Bible but saw God, good, and evil in non-salvation terms. New Thought words and phrases like higher power, cosmic consciousness, fourth dimension, and Universal Mind filtered into the A.A. stream. The significant New Thought expositors included Mary Baker Eddy, Waldo Trine, William James, Emmanuel Movement writers, and Emmet Fox. See Dick B. *The Books Early AAs Read for Spiritual Growth, 7th ed; When Early AAs Were Cured and Why; Dr. Bob and His Library; Good Morning: Quiet Time, Morning Watch, Meditation, and Early A.A.; God and Alcoholism.*

Number Fourteen: The Bible. There is scarcely a one of the foregoing thirteen examples that didn't involve the Bible in one way or another. I have written so much about the Bible and early A.A. that I want to do little more here than point to my titles which cover the subject like a blanket. See Dick B. *The Good Book and The Big Book: A.A.'s Roots in the Bible; The Good Book-Big Book Guidebook; Why Early A.A. Succeeded; When Early AAs Were Cured and Why; The Akron Genesis of Alcoholics Anonymous; Turning Point; God and Alcoholism; Cured; The Oxford Group and Alcoholics Anonymous; New Light on Alcoholism; By the Power of God; The Golden Text of A.A.; The First Nationwide A.A. History Conference; Twelve Steps for You; A New Way Out.*

The Plan Bill Incorporated from these Sources

Conversion

Bill accepted and adopted as the requisite target and solution for alcoholism the theory of Dr. Carl Gustav Jung that a person with the mind of a chronic alcoholic could be cured by a conversion experience. Bill sought and experienced such a conversion at the altar of Calvary Rescue Mission. Shortly thereafter at Towns Hospital, Bill called out to the Great Physician for help and had what he called his "hot flash" experience. The former at the altar could be equated with Akron's "real surrenders." The latter was simply not part of Akron's program.

Validation of Conversions

Bill felt he had the validity of such conversions confirmed in the accounts by William James in his *Varieties of Religious Experiences*, which Bill studied. Many of the accounts by James covered conversions at the altar of a Mission. Bill also felt that Professor James had spelled out the necessity for "calamity," or "deflation at depth" as a prerequisite to surrenders.

Admission of defeat

In his own personal story, Bill confessed that he had been licked—that alcohol had become his master. He also drew on the remarks of Dr. William Duncan Silkworth that real alcoholics were suffering from an obsession of the mind which led them to drink and an allergy of the body which prevented them from moderate drinking. Further, Bill had heard from Oxford Group stories that many had preceded their "surrenders" with the use of the "manage me" prayer. In one form or another, both Frank Buchman and Sam Shoemaker were involved in the use of the prayer, "O God, manage me because I can't manage myself." The prayer appears also in Anne Smith's Journal. And taking all these contributing elements, Bill fashioned his First Step to suggest that alcoholics needed to admit they were "powerless" over alcohol, and that their lives had become unmanageable. The "powerless" idea seemed a reconstruction of the "I was licked" language designed to lead to Bill's theory that you moved from "powerless" to a "power greater than yourself" which he later proclaimed as the main purpose of his book. Akron, of course, simply began by demanding a belief in God, coupled with an acceptance of Christ.

Coming to believe, and finding God.

Dr. Bob adamantly insisted on a belief in the Creator as a prerequisite to cure. He himself had always believed. Wilson, on the other hand, went through a period in his life with depressions and drinking that left him thinking he was a "conservative atheist." And Rev. Sam Shoemaker had just the ticket for Bill. Shoemaker had written extensively on the need for man to find God through a vital religious experience. He said you needed Jesus Christ and a new birth for this to happen. Shoemaker strongly held to the idea that obedience to God was the organ of spiritual knowledge. He predicated his thinking on his favorite verse, John 7:17—"If any man will do his will, he shall know of the doctrine, whether it be of God, or whether I speak of myself," said Jesus. To Shoemaker, this meant that one could come to believe in and know God by taking action—doing God's will. Sam's apologia was titled, "I stand by Door," which meant pointing the way through the door to finding God. Hence Bill fashioned his Second Step with Shoemaker ideas that one could "find God" based on the necessity for believing that God—whom Shoemaker also dubbed a "power greater than ourselves" could restore the alcoholic to sanity and hence abstinence.

The decision to surrender.

Dr. Bob simply had a newcomer confirm his belief in God and establish a relationship with him through confessing Christ. "Conversion" was a done deal in Akron at that point. On the other hand, Bill adopted Shoemaker's thesis that "finding God" and being "born again" was an action process. And the action started with a *decision—something Bill later described in Step Three..* At one point, Shoemaker simply suggested a "decision" to cast one's will and life on God. Bill adopted that as the first action step and coupled it with a surrender prayer that adopted Sam's language from the Lord's prayer—"Thy will be done." But Bill also threw in the mix a good deal of Oxford Group/Shoemaker thinking that "self-centeredness" was a hindrance to successful action. "Self is not God, and God is God," said Sam. "Ego-centricity" became the named adversary.

Inventory of sins

There was strong language in Oxford Group writings to the effect that "sin" was anything that blocked you from God and other people. These activists believed that sins needed to be inventoried in writing and used to test the "moral standards" of the person seeking a relationship with God. Originally, the test was based on one's adherence to the Four Absolutes—honesty, purity, unselfishness, and love. Dr. Bob favored these standards. Bill Wilson did not; and Bill designated from Oxford Group language four items that were to be used as yardsticks—resentment, self-seeking, dishonesty, and fear. Coupled with these was a listing of how and where these identified sins had harmed someone. The concept came largely from the Sermon on the Mount. Bill dubbed it as Step Four.

Confession of sins

To get rid of sins blocking you from God, said the Oxford Group, you needed to inventory them and then fully, honestly, and completely admit them to yourself, another human being, and God. They based their thinking on James 5:16 though its language did not exactly square with their "admitted to God, another human being, and ourselves" the behavior. This action process was dubbed Step Five.

Conviction of Sins

The Oxford Group used the "Five C's" in its life-changing action program. They were: Confidence, Confession, Conviction, Conversion, and Continuance. And the writings of Anne Smith and Lois Wilson frequently refer to being "convicted" of this or that wrongful thinking or conduct. Become "convicted" or "convinced" that one needed to change, to eliminate, and to be free of the items inventories and confessed was a long-time Biblical idea. And, though few—including Bill—seemed to know what the step meant, Bill dubbed the process Step Six and simply said one needed to be entirely ready to change.

Conversion

In Biblical language, sins were remitted when one confessed Jesus as Saviour because Jesus had, as a substitute, paid the price for the sins. Hence the conversion alone did the job. Romans 5:1 informed believers they were justified (acquitted) by faith and had peace with God through their Lord Jesus Christ. Romans 6:22 told them that "now being made free from sin, and become servants to God,: they had their fruit unto holiness." Romans 8:1 that "there is therefore no condemnation to them which are in Christ Jesus, who walk not after the flesh but after the Spirit. 1 Corinthians 6:11 had told them of many sinners but said "And such were some of you: but ye are washed, but ye are sanctified, but ye are justified in the name of the Lord Jesus, and by the Spirit of our God." Galatians 3:22 "But the scripture hath concluded all under sin, that the promise by faith of Jesus Christ might be given to them that believe." That Wilson took his Seventh Step idea from the Biblical assurance that Christians had been bought with a price, he clung to the idea that action was still required for a conversion to be complete. Bill covered believing in Step Two a la Shoemaker. Bill covered "surrender" in Step Three a la Shoemaker. Yet he seemed compelled to add in "conversion" through the Seventh Step in order quietly to incorporate this 5 C concept. In any event, Bill wrote the Step and the prayer, but Shoemaker wrote that this process could be likened to James 4:10, where the believer humbles himself in the sight of the Lord, and the Lord lifts him up. Shoemaker wrote that we all need a kind of "divine derrick" to lift us out of the mire.

Continuance

Though the Oxford Group idea, taken from the Bible, was that conversion was complete, they also recognized that one was as prone to sin and blocks to God as always. They fashioned the idea that he had to "conserve" his new-found state and "continue" to improve his relationship with the Creator. But how?

The answer was an Oxford Group answer, based on ideas readily found in the Sermon on the Mount. The believer was to *continue* to clean house.

The Restitution job: And the first order of business was to take care of past wrongs—not as a guilty person, but as one doing God's will in agreeing with his adversary quickly and restoring to another anything wrongfully taken. The process was covered in Bill's Steps Eight and Nine. And "restitution" was clearly an Oxford Group "must." Bill wrote his "promises" that before one was half-way through, he would begin to know a new freedom.

The Continuing watchfulness and corrections: What of new temptations, new resentments, new fears, new dishonesty, new selfish behavior? Shoemaker wrote that the devil comes back along familiar paths. Hence one was to "continue" to look for the behavior that might again block him from God. The way of continuance was to use the tools of the first nine steps. And a careful reading of the Step Ten language in the Big Book will show that it applies the removal-of-sin techniques in the first nine steps to daily watchfulness and remedial action in Step Ten.

The Daily Fellowship with God and His son: What of "back-sliding?" Frank Amos used this biblical term. The Oxford Group might not have used that phrase, but it pointed up the need for continuing spiritual contact and growth. You are either growing or dying might be a way of putting it. And the way to continuing renewals was through Quiet Time. In Akron, this meant Bible study, prayer, seeking God's guidance, reading religious literature, fellowship, and witness. In the Big Book, these Biblical trappings were omitted. In fact, the Oxford Group quiet time ideas were rephrased, watered down, and rendered partially impotent. Whether talking about the evening inventory, or the morning devotions, or the daily studies, or the means of dealing with anxieties, Wilson was far off base in employing the power of God in the process. For example, in the last portion of his Eleventh Step discussion, Wilson simply advocated saying, "Thy will be done." As if that acceptance idea would somehow bring peace and victory.

Not so in the Bible where Ephesians Chapter Six points up the continuing need to put on the whole armour of God and recognize the power and presence of the Adversary.

Bill's Other Revisions of the Akron Program

To make sure the complete history of the Big Book and Twelve Steps is on the table, we should add some additional ideas Bill added to the original program.

New Thought ideas and phrases: Bill and Bob both read New Thought writings. These included the works of Mary Baker Eddy, Ralph Waldo Trine, William James, Charles and Cora Filmore, the Emanuel Movement writers, Glenn Clark, and Emmet Fox. Just how did these writings impact on Bill's writings? We do know that the compromise words for God such as Higher Power, Universal Mind, Infinite Power, Great Reality, and the like come from these writers. We do know that the Akron requirement of a genuine Christian conversion does not exist in the Big Book and certainly was spurned by Emmet Fox who wrote that the Bible contained no support for salvation and had no theology. We know that such expressions as "fourth dimension," "cosmic consciousness," and "conscious contact with God" not only have no Biblical roots, but seem related either to New Thought writings or even to the spiritualist and psychic adventures of Bill Wilson.

Biblical ideas eliminated: Bill certainly declined to mention the countless Biblical ideas that underlay his own story, the solution, the action steps, the descriptions of the Creator, and even give attributions for direct Bible quotes from James, the Lord's Prayer, and elsewhere. Jesus Christ was intentionally disposed of as a factor in A.A. recovery. The Holy Spirit seems unmentioned. And the ideas of Bible study meetings, prayer meetings, conversion meetings, Quiet Times, reading of Christian literature, and religious comradeship have vanished. So have any specific references to Carl Jung, Frank Buchman, Samuel Shoemaker, the Oxford Group, and the Bible itself. And there are plenty of similar omissions, revisions, and deletions—all having roots in the intentional revision of A.A. principles and practices.

Interjection of Richard Peabody negatives: I fail to understand one major revision Bill made. Bill Wilson, Dr. Bob, Bill Dotson, and a host of the original pioneers all said specifically they had been cured of alcoholism by their Creator. So did a host of commentators such as Elrick Davis, Liberty Magazine, and Paul de Kruif, not to mention the clergy that sprang to endorse Bill's new movement. What topped the list, however, were the dozens of newspaper, magazine, and periodical statements around the entire United States where all kinds of A.A. members were proclaiming their cure, their healings at God's hands, and their healings. Nonetheless, when an irreligious lay therapist who died drunk stated that there was no cure for alcoholism and laid on alcoholics the curse: "Once an alcoholic, always an alcoholic," Bill seized these ideas and ignored the views of Carl Jung, William James, William D. Silkworth, Sam Shoemaker, Oxford Group activists and the very physician quotes in the Big Book that alcoholics were 100% hopeless without Divine Aid.

Lois Wilson's universalism statement: Just what prompted Lois Wilson to declare and believe that AAs had somehow sometime agreed that their program should be a universal one "since not all drunks were Christians" is something we do not know. But that view has dominated thinking among AAs with increasing force as the years have passed since the Akron Christian Fellowship successes.

Bill's Deep Depressions and the Multiplication of Diversionary Programs

Bill Wilson suffered from deep depressions all of his life. They began in his youth with the separation of his parents and the untimely death of his first love. They continued through his drinking years. And they became virtually totally disabling beginning in 1942 through the year 1955. The situation is no secret. It is covered in A.A.'s *Pass It On*. It is discussed in detail by Mel B. in his *My Search for Bill W.* And recent biographers have given it even further play. It will be covered in my forthcoming title *The Conversion of Bill W.*

The important point is that A.A. began to change dramatically almost the moment Bill published the Big Book in the Spring of 1939. The events transpired as follows.

Clarence Snyder and Cleveland A.A. Perhaps it all started constructively in May, 1939 when Clarence Snyder took the Bible, the Oxford Group Four Absolutes, the Big Book, and the Twelve Steps to Cleveland and made hay with the old and the new, retaining strong ties to both. Cleveland's groups grew from one to thirty in a year. The success rate soared to 93%. And Clarence developed guides to taking the steps and sponsorship. See Three Clarence Snyder Sponsee Old-timers and Their Wives: *Our A.A. Legacy to the Faith Community: A Twelve-Step Guide for Those Who Want to Believe*. Comp. ed. by Dick B. Winter Park, FL: Came to Believe Publications, 2005.

Dr, Bob, Sister Ignatia, and St. Thomas Hospital: In 1940, Akron began to be focused on hospitalization and Twelfth-stepping as part of the work by Dr. Bob and Sister Ignatia at St. Thomas Hospital in Akron. This work retained the important hospitalization of old. But Sister Ignatia added some new approaches, and both Dr. Bob and Anne Smith were moving toward their declining years in energy and effort. The Ignatia story is well covered in Mary C. Darrah. *Sister Ignatia: Angel of Alcoholics Anonymous.* Chicago: Loyola University Press, 1992; and, while it cannot be said that the A.A. program thereby changed, it does seem that a stint with Bob, Ignatia, and St. Thomas might have inclined St. Thomas patients to believe they had completed their rehabilitation even though Akron Group Number One was still meeting, and Dr. Bob was still active.

Enter four new influences. Their respective consequences and works are covered elsewhere, but each brought substantial changes to A.A. itself:

(1) Father Ed Dowling, S.J., entered the scene in late 1940; he communicated with Bill for the next twenty years. Their subject matter: Bill's "second conversion" when he did a "fifth step" with Dowling, Dowling's view of the significance of the Exercises of St. Ignatius, and a steady flow of letters. See Robert Fitzgerald. *The Soul of Sponsorship: The Friendship of Fr. Ed Dowling, S.J., and Bill Wilson in Letters*. Hazelden, 1995. But, by 1942, Bill had gone into a deep, severe, almost immobilizing thirteen year depression. And still other leaders and programs were, for whatever reason, attempting to fill the gap.

(2) Richmond Walker had a spotty past as a recycled drunk. He gained an interest in the Oxford Group and its literature as early as 1934. He joined the Oxford Group in 1939 to get sober, but didn't succeed for much over two years. But he gained extensive knowledge of Oxford Group ideas In May of 1942, he entered A.A. and was involved in three very influential literary works. He worked with a devotional titled *God Calling*, which had been edited by Oxford Group writer A.A. Russell. In 1945, a Massachusetts A.A group published Walker's *For Drunks Only* which was filled with Oxford Group ideas, A.A. principles, and sobriety suggestions. He offered it to A.A. for publication and was declined. In 1948, Walker worked with *God Calling* and converted it to a recovery devotional that has sold in the millions, though also declined by A.A. itself. That devotional is titled *Twenty-Four Hours Book*

(3) Father Ralph Pfau Ralph was the first Roman Catholic priest to get sober in Alcoholics Anonymous (he came in on November 10, 1943), and under the pen name which he chose to use, Father John Doe, he wrote his fourteen Golden Books back in the 1940's and 50's and early 60's. They are still being read and used by A.A.'s today: *Spiritual Side* (1947), *Tolerance* (1948), *Attitudes* (1949), and others.

They were coming out once a year at the beginning. Then Pfau changed his writing and published three much longer books, including *Sobriety and Beyond* (1955).

(4) Ed Webster: In 1946, in Minneapolis, Ed Webster published *The Little Red Book* under the sponsorship of the A.A. Nicollet Group. Its title was "An Interpretation of the Twelve Steps." Ed had the help and support of Dr. Bob, who gave numerous suggestions for wording various passages. Ed also wrote *Stools and Bottles* (1955), *Barroom Reveries* (1958) and *Our Devilish Alcoholic Personalities* (in 1970, just a year before his death).

Bill's *Twelve Steps and Twelve Traditions*: When Bill finally pulled out of his depression, Anne Smith was dead, Dr. Bob was dead, the reigns of A.A. were becoming the property of New York, and Bill had set about writing a whole new program in his book *Twelve Steps and Twelve Traditions*. It was heavily edited by two Roman Catholic Jesuit priests who purportedly sought to eliminate Oxford Group thoughts from its content. Bill also introduced a second edition of the basic text and adopted "spiritual awakening" as the target of the steps—leaving conversion, religious experience, and spiritual experience in the dust bin. He completely replaced "conversion" with a psychological conclusion that, for most AAs, a mere personality change sufficient to overcome the "disease" of alcoholism was all that was required for recovery.

Finally, recovery centers and literature substantially pre-empted doctrinal literature publication and distribution. But, as all the foregoing developments occurred, the A.A. success rates became observably more and more dismal—dropping from its original rate of at least 75% to about 5%.

And these changes—one and all—provide solid reasons for returning to, re-examining, and learning early ideas and history.

AA OF AKRON rides again through its four later pamphlets commissioned by Dr. Bob

I don't think anything surprised me more as an AA from the West Coast than finding the four AA OF AKRON pamphlets on sale at the

Akron A.A. Intergroup Office--pamphlets originally commissioned by Dr. Bob. They had apparently been around for years. They were filled with the kind of Akron A.A. I've described above. They quoted the Bible, recommended prayer, discussed the importance of God, and did so in the context of the Twelve Steps. Yet how in the world did these gems come into being when their contents were virtually unknown where I came from? They seemed at first to be the product or property of some "clandestine A.A." until I learned what I know today—that they closely resembled the Frank Amos summary of early A.A.

I can't say and do not know how much research has been done on their origins. But this much has been suggested. Dr. Bob felt that the program in the Big Book was not easy for "blue collar" AAs to deal with. He asked Evan W. to prepare some practical guides. And four emerged. For those who have become acquainted with early A.A. in Akron, there's not a surprise in them even though two of the four I own were republished, respectively in 1989 and 1993, while the other two were republished in October, 1997.

Treat yourself to this A.A. program material. Program principles and practices that were *not written by Bill W.,* that square with the A.A. that Frank Amos summarized, that frequently quote the Bible—just as Dr. Bob did, and that I described in detail above. And let's look at the general ideas in each of the pamphlets, one by one:

Spiritual Milestones in Alcoholics Anonymous

At the outset, this pamphlet asks and answers the following:

> But, asks the alcoholic, where can I find a simple, step-by-step religious guide? The Ten Commandments give us a set of Thou Shalts and Thou Shalt Nots; the Twelve Steps of AA give us a program of dynamic action; but what about a spiritual guide? Of course the answer is that by following the Ten Commandments and Twelve Steps to the letter we automatically lead a spiritual life, whether or not we recognize it.

Then the pamphlet says: "Here, however, is a set of suggestions, couched in the simplest of language:

1 – Eliminate sin from our lives.
2 – Develop humility
3 – Constantly pray to God for guidance.
4 – Practice charity.
5 – Meditate frequently on our newly found blessings, giving honest thanks for them.
6 – Take God into our confidence in all our acts.
7 – Seek the companionship of others who are seeking a spiritual life.

And the explanatory discussions of these seven points frequently mention God, Christianity, the Bible, and prayer. The pamphlet gives several illustrations of how men have found God. It concludes with the Prayer of St. Francis of Assisi.

A Manual for Alcoholics Anonymous.

This guide picks up the trail where *Spiritual Milestones* left off. It addresses the newcomer, hospitalization, sponsors, visiting the hospital, and what the newcomer must do on his discharge. He is told to read the Bible and give particular attention to the Sermon on the Mount, Book of James, 1 Corinthians 13, and the Twenty-third and Ninety-first Psalms. The guide suggests a prayer life for each and every day. Then it describes the thrill of helping someone else. Citing Matthew 6:34 of the Sermon on the Mount, it suggests day by day time progress and acquiring health "one day at a time." It quotes Step Twelve as a "Spiritual Experience," not the "Awakening" Bill was soon to substitute as the result of taking the steps.

Second Reader for Alcoholics Anonymous

Its primary topic is, WHAT IS THERE IN AA FOR ME BESIDES SOBRIETY. And the article discusses four items: "Work, Play, Love, and Religion"—substituting A.A. for the latter. It contends that the good active AA is practicing Christianity whether he knows it or not. It devotes a paragraph to the Bible accounts that children loved for years: The Lord's Prayer, David and Goliath and Samson, Adam and Eve in the Garden, the Prodigal Son, and the Good Samaritan. And it lays out some very practical and purposeful ways of sharing a story in A.A. meetings.

A Guide to the Twelve Steps of Alcoholics Anonymous

With this fourth pamphlet, Akron AA completes the circuit of A.A. activity. It offers the following as a simplified, condensed form of the complete program:

- We honestly admitted we were powerless over alcohol and sincerely wanted to do something about it. In other words, we admitted we were whipped and had a genuine desire to QUIT FOR GOOD.
- We asked and received help from a power greater than ourselves and another human. (NOTE: In almost all cases that power is called God. It is, however, God as WE UNDERSTAND HIM. . . .)
- We cleaned up our lives, paid our debts, righted wrongs.
- We carried our new way of life to others desperately in need of it.

The pamphlet discusses each of the Twelve Steps individually. It concludes with these rules for living.

- Remember that you an alcoholic, and but one drink away from drunkenness again.
- Remember that you are completely dependent on God as you understand Him.
- Remember to keep your thinking straight.
- Remember that a wrong act will play on your mind until you either do something to rectify it or get drunk.
- Remember that defects will creep into your life if given half a chance.
- Remember that if only through gratitude, we must help others in order to help ourselves.

Is It Any Wonder!

Just look at the road traveled in A.A. between 1935 and 1955. Just look at how the early Akron A.A. precepts perished a little more along each step of the road. And then ask if it's any wonder that today's people don't even know their history, and perhaps don't even want to know it.

But our educational target is the child of God in A.A.—the Christian, the believer, if you wish—who is awash in authoritative talk about spirituality, higher powers, powerlessness, personality changes, and experiences. It is he who needs to be reached with the simplicity of the early Christian Fellowship program. He has as much at stake in that program as any other person in A.A. It concerns his life, his freedom, and his happiness which were spiraling down the tube in his drinking years. And he has as much need and right as any person in A.A. to know that his own beliefs—when used to deliver him from the power of darkness—were the very beliefs that delivered early AAs from the curse of alcoholism. It was alcohol that was the enemy and the key. And the early pioneers found out how to defeat that enemy and turn the lock with the help of Almighty God.

Part 4: How Adding A History Element to Recovery Can Help the Newcomer Today

Simple Elements of the Programs of Its Precursors

Take a look at our descriptions of the heart of the powerhouse early programs that preceded A.A.

The Salvation Army operated on ideas of abstinence, reliance on the Creator, salvation, obedience to God's commandments with elimination of sin, and growth in fellowship with the Father and His son through Bible and prayer. They also provided shelter, food, and assistance in living. Then came intensive work with the poor, the criminals, and the broken-hearted outcasts, who were pulled out of the slums and enlisted for similar work themselves.

The Rescue Missions were little different. Their focus was, of course, on "soup, soap, and salvation," and they provided food, shelter, counseling, and material needs. But their focus was on the mission service and the altar call. What did this countenance: Acceptance of the Lord, Bible reading, prayer, singing, hymns, and brotherly support. Many there also remained to help others.

The YMCA focus was on evangelism, Christianity, and personal work.

The Oxford Group stressed belief in God, obedience to His will, elimination of sin, continuing life change that resulted in better relations with others, Bible, prayer, seeking God's guidance in Quiet Time, restitution, fellowship, loyalty, and witness.

The United Christian Endeavor Society was not focused on alcoholism. But it certainly brought to the table the importance of confessing Jesus Christ, Bible study, prayer meetings, conversion of others, reading and discussing Christian literature, Quiet Hour, religious comradeship, support of church, love and service. And these very ideas presented to Dr. Bob in his youth became the heart of the "spiritual" renewal that accompanied Akron's specific development of a movement to help drunks.

The Essentials that Akron Borrowed from the Foregoing Sources

Abstinence and Resisting Temptation;

Reliance on the Creator;

Establishing sonship through a New Birth;

Obedience to God's commandments – the walk of love and elimination of sinful conduct;

Growth in Fellowship with the Father through Bible study, Prayer, Communicating with God and His Son, and Reading of Christian literature;

Love and service to others that glorifies the Creator – fellowship, witness, intensive work with the poor, sick, and broken-hearted.

The Prescription of Two Well-Known Recovery Workers

William Duncan Silkworth, M.D. Silkworth was Bill Wilson's physician, a long-time treatment specialist for the chronic alcoholic, and a faithful friend of A.A. itself. In a little-known article published in the Journal-Lancet on July 27, 1939, Dr. Silkworth wrote about the essential features of a new approach to psychotherapy that had produced remarkable results and promised much for the future. See Dale Mitchell. Silkworth *The Little Doctor Who Loved Drunks: The Biography of William Duncan Silkworth, M.D.* MN: Hazelden, 2002. Silkworth said: "The essential features of this new approach, without psychological embellishment, are:

1. The ex-alcoholics capitalize upon a fact which they have so well demonstrated, namely, that one alcoholic can secure the confidence of another in a way and to a degree

almost impossible of attainment by a non-alcoholic outsider.

2. After having fully identified themselves with their "prospect" by a recital of symptoms, behavior, anecdotes, etc., these men allow the patient to draw the inference that if he is seriously alcoholic, there may be no hope for him save a spiritual experience. They cite their own cases and quote medical opinion to prove their point. If the patient insists he is not alcoholic to that degree, they recommend that he try to stay sober in his own way. Usually, the patient agrees at once. If he does not, a few more painful relapses often convince him.

3. Once the patient agrees that he is powerless, he finds himself in a serious dilemma. He sees clearly that he must have a spiritual experience or be destroyed by alcohol.

4. This dilemma brings about a crisis in the patient's life. He finds himself in a situation which, he believes, cannot be untangled by human means. He has been placed in this position by another alcoholic who has recovered through a spiritual experience. This peculiar ability which an alcoholic who has recovered exercises upon one who has not recovered, is the main secret of the unprecedented success which these men and women are having. They can penetrate and carry conviction where the physician or clergyman cannot. Under these conditions, the patient turns to religion with an entire willingness and readily accepts, without reservation, a simple religious proposal. He is then able to acquire much more than a set of religious beliefs; he undergoes a profound mental and emotional change common to religious "experience." (See William James' Varieties of Religious Experience). Then, too, the patient's hope is renewed and his imagination is fired by the idea of membership in a group of ex-alcoholics where he will be enabled to save the lives and homes of those who have suffered as he has suffered.

5. The fellowship is entirely indifferent concerning the individual manner of spiritual approach so long as the patient is willing to turn his life and his problems over to the care of his Creator. The patient may picture the Deity in any way he likes. No effort whatever is made to convert him to some particular faith or creed. Many creeds are represented among the group and the greatest harmony prevails. It is emphasized that the fellowship is non-sectarian and that the patient is entirely free to follow his own inclination. Not a trace of aggressive evangelism is exhibited.

6. If the patient indicates a willingness to go on, a suggestion is made that he do certain things which are obviously good psychology, good morals and good religion, regardless of creed:

    a. That he make a moral appraisal of himself, and confidentially discuss his findings with a competent person whom he trusts.
    b. That he try to adjust bad personal relationships, setting right, so far as possible, such wrongs as he may have done in the past.
    c. That he recommit himself daily, or hourly if need be, to God's care and direction, asking for strength.
    d. That if possible, he attend weekly meetings of the fellowship and actively lend a hand with alcoholic newcomers.

Jerry G. Dunn, author of *God is for the Alcoholic:* Some years ago, the proprietor of a Christian bookstore gave me a copy of Jerry Dunn's book, but I never read it. Much later, I was asked to speak at the first International Convention of Alcoholics Victorious. And Jerry Dunn was the other speaker. Gnarled, venerable, and powerful in his speech, Jerry was truly a heavy hitter. I think he was some 80 years old when he spoke at this convention. He'd been a real alcoholic, served his time in prison, accepted Christ, been in A.A., and then spent many years as a lay preacher helping alcoholics.

Recently, I have read, re-read, and quoted his book many times in connection with various titles I've been writing. And what struck me here were the specific tips that Jerry laid out in his book for helping alcoholics—tips that match the procedures outlined above, and tips that have produced the same successes. See Jerry G. Dunn. *God is for the Alcoholic.* Chicago: The Moody Bible Institute of Chicago, 1965.

Beginning one segment of his book, Dunn says: "Every problem of man has a spiritual solution. The ever increasing problem of alcoholism is no exception. God has provided a way of escape" (p. 79). In Part II, Jerry then spells out in five chapters, Five Ways to Help the Alcoholic. The material is lengthy and meaty. So I'll merely provide an outline. And the five ways are:

1. Use Untapped Resources: The first way, says Jerry, is to pray for the alcoholic. And he lays out these ground rules: (a) Be sure you are a member of God's family because prayer is a privilege and duty of the children of God. (b) Stand on God's Promise to Answer Prayer. (c) Regularly observe private prayer, getting alone with God; and practice public prayer in the prayer meeting at church. (d) Remember you are the supply line. You cry out to God. That sets His forces to work. He sends His power by the Holy Spirit to us and through us to the individual (e) Did you ask—presenting with confidence any petition that is according to His will (f) Are you expecting an answer?

2. Presenting the Gospel: "The gospel of Christ. . . is the power of God unto salvation to everyone that believeth: to the Jew first, and also to the Greed" (Romans 1:16). (a) First Things First: Give the alcoholic love and comfort by putting your arm around the alcoholic and telling him that God loves him, praying for him as you send him on his way, perhaps, to get medical attention. (b) You have to throw away the clock when you're dealing with an alcoholic. (c) God's way is basic. (d) Christianity is a life to live. (d) Christianity is a new life.

3. Fellowship: A.A. has made fellowship a cornerstone in their efforts to help the individual. Of course, fellowship is

a two-way street. It must be offered, received, and returned. (a) Use the Samaritan principle. (b) Fellowship needs to come from family, church, friends, and associates. (c) He cites the short, helpful creed of Alcoholics Victorious.

4. Long-Suffering: The need for (a) patience. (b) applying the Prodigal Son principle.

5. Firmness: (a) Letting the alcoholic stand on his own two feet. (b) Make ground rules. (c) Protect your interests. (d) Do not do for him what he should do. (e) Ask advice. (f) The actions of the alcoholic speak louder than his words. (g) Break community dependence in the institutionalized alcoholic, the probationary alcoholic, and the rehabilitated alcoholic.

The Bottom Line is Helping the Alcoholic Who Still Suffers to be Cured by God

You can see that there is no simple way of dealing with and restoring a sick alcoholic.

He is a person who needs to be qualified as a real alcoholic, as one who understands what a real alcoholic is, as one who admits without hesitation that he qualifies, and as one who will do whatever it takes to get well. Only then can your efforts bear fruit.

You can see that neither Akron nor its powerhouse predecessors pussyfooted about the Creator. They pointed, as Ebby Thacher did, to what God had done for them. They manifested that victory by their presence and language. They did not compromise in their talk about God, about His son, about conversion, about the Bible, and about the need for living a new life that God has made possible. Compromise on God? No. Substitute gods? No. Apologize for your belief? No. Minimize the importance of Divine Aid? No. Skip the role of Jesus Christ as the way, the truth, and the life? No. Skirt the study of the Bible? No. Avoid firm instructions about prayer? No. Lay it on the line the way the pioneers did—God either is, or He isn't, God cured our founders. The founders knew they needed to witness to those facts in order for the newcomer to understand what a "spiritual" program really meant.

There was no pussyfooting about abstinence and resisting temptation. You can't make the alcoholic quit if he doesn't want to. But you can make clear that quitting means quitting for good, forever, for always. Also, that the surest way back to the bottle or the needle is to follow the old paths that led you there in the first place.

Emphasis on God as a Father who wants us to become His children and tells us how. Also on how He loves, forgives, heals, supplies, guides, and protects His kids. Also on His expectation that we will obey His commandments and rules by learning them, understanding them, and following them—whether they pertain to love of God and others or to eliminating harm to others.

Show them the Adversary, the spiritual battle, and the tools by which the spiritual battle must be won—as outlined in Ephesians Chapter 6.

Stress the need for constant, daily, serious spiritual work through reading God's Word, praying to God, listening for His voice, and following His precepts. "Meditation" is not humming. It's studying, pondering, focusing on what God has to say and how to understand Him.

Hugging is not just for babies. AAs hug. Just as contact with a pet warms the heart and elicits happy responses, so does tangible contact with another alcoholic—whether in greeting, support, sympathy, condolence, or joy.

Fellowship keeps the embers glowing. Departing from the gang of believes is often the beginning of return to unbelievers.

Witnessing is a pleasure, a duty, a protection, and a service. God expects you to present the Gospel to others. And you have a duty to present it accurately, lovingly, and carefully.

History Backs Up the Promises of Victory

The simple program of early A.A. came from simple, effective programs of organizations like the Salvation Army, Rescue Missions, the YMCA, the Oxford Group, and United Christian Endeavor. It inherited the structure of Congregationalism—self autonomy, self government, self support, and freedom from higher decision makers. Its precepts merely required love and service by successful people cured of their terrible curse of alcoholism. Its program merely called for them to urge abstinence, warn about temptation, stress reliance on God, make conversion available, insist on principles of obedience to God's word, stress growth through Bible study and prayer and literature, and joining in intense work with newcomers that glorifies God. It worked. It will work today. But only if people know what it was and believe.

Hindrances Need to be Understood and Rejected

Christians in today's Twelve Step Fellowships need to know their Christian roots. They need to stand firm on their own beliefs. They need to reject or ignore compromise solutions and idolatry. They need to reclaim their own victories through Christ.

They'll stand, stick and grow as they strive to:

End rock-throwing by AAs and religious
End idolatry and evil expressions contradicting the Bible

Emphasize history, wholeness, cure

Always to join Dr. Bob in His answers to questions about the program—"What does the Good Book say."

END

Gloria Dei

Appendix

New Testament Healing Records Categorized

Dead or Nearly Dead People Made Alive or Healed

Matthew 9
18 While he spake these things unto them, behold, there came a certain ruler, and worshipped him, saying, My daughter is even now dead: but come and lay thy hand upon her, and she shall live.
19 And Jesus arose, and followed him, and so did his disciples.

23 And when Jesus came into the ruler's house, and saw the minstrels and the people making a noise,
24 He said unto them, Give place: for the maid is not dead, but sleepeth. And they laughed him to scorn.
25 But when the people were put forth, he went in, and took her by the hand, and the maid arose.
26 And the fame hereof went abroad into all that land.

Mark 5
21 And when Jesus was passed over again by ship unto the other side, much people gathered unto him: and he was nigh unto the sea.
22 And, behold, there cometh one of the rulers of the synagogue, Jairus by name; and when he saw him, he fell at his feet,
23 And besought him greatly, saying, My little daughter lieth at the point of death: I pray thee, come and lay thy hands on her, that she may be healed; and she shall live.
24 And Jesus went with him; and much people followed him, and thronged him.

35 While he yet spake, there came from the ruler of the synagogue's house certain which said, Thy daughter is dead: why troublest thou the Master any further?
36 As soon as Jesus heard the word that was spoken, he saith unto the ruler of the synagogue, Be not afraid, only believe.
37 And he suffered no man to follow him, save Peter, and James, and

John the brother of James.

³⁸ And he cometh to the house of the ruler of the synagogue, and seeth the tumult, and them that wept and wailed greatly.

³⁹ And when he was come in, he saith unto them, Why make ye this ado, and weep? the damsel is not dead, but sleepeth.

⁴⁰ And they laughed him to scorn. But when he had put them all out, he taketh the father and the mother of the damsel, and them that were with him, and entereth in where the damsel was lying.

⁴¹ And he took the damsel by the hand, and said unto her, Talitha cumi; which is, being interpreted, Damsel, I say unto thee, arise.

⁴² And straightway the damsel arose, and walked; for she was of the age of twelve years. And they were astonished with a great astonishment.

⁴³ And he charged them straitly that no man should know it; and commanded that something should be given her to eat.

Luke 7

¹ Now when he had ended all his sayings in the audience of the people, he entered into Capernaum.

² And a certain centurion's servant, who was dear unto him, was sick, and ready to die.

³ And when he heard of Jesus, he sent unto him the elders of the Jews, beseeching him that he would come and heal his servant.

⁴ And when they came to Jesus, they besought him instantly, saying, That he was worthy for whom he should do this:

⁵ For he loveth our nation, and he hath built us a synagogue.

⁶ Then Jesus went with them. And when he was now not far from the house, the centurion sent friends to him, saying unto him, Lord, trouble not thyself: for I am not worthy that thou shouldest enter under my roof:

⁷ Wherefore neither thought I myself worthy to come unto thee: but say in a word, and my servant shall be healed.

⁸ For I also am a man set under authority, having under me soldiers, and I say unto one, Go, and he goeth; and to another, Come, and he cometh; and to my servant, Do this, and he doeth it.

⁹ When Jesus heard these things, he marvelled at him, and turned him about, and said unto the people that followed him, I say unto you, I have not found so great faith, no, not in Israel.

¹⁰ And they that were sent, returning to the house, found the servant whole that had been sick.

Luke 7

¹¹ And it came to pass the day after, that he went into a city called Nain; and many of his disciples went with him, and much people.
¹² Now when he came nigh to the gate of the city, behold, there was a dead man carried out, the only son of his mother, and she was a widow: and much people of the city was with her.
¹³ And when the Lord saw her, he had compassion on her, and said unto her, Weep not.
¹⁴ And he came and touched the bier: and they that bare him stood still. And he said, Young man, I say unto thee, Arise.
¹⁵ And he that was dead sat up, and began to speak. And he delivered him to his mother.
¹⁶ And there came a fear on all: and they glorified God, saying, That a great prophet is risen up among us; and, That God hath visited his people.
¹⁷ And this rumour of him went forth throughout all Judaea, and throughout all the region round about.

Luke 8

⁴⁰ And it came to pass, that, when Jesus was returned, the people gladly received him: for they were all waiting for him.
⁴¹ And, behold, there came a man named Jairus, and he was a ruler of the synagogue: and he fell down at Jesus' feet, and besought him that he would come into his house:
⁴² For he had one only daughter, about twelve years of age, and she lay a dying. But as he went the people thronged him.

⁴⁹ While he yet spake, there cometh one from the ruler of the synagogue's house, saying to him, Thy daughter is dead; trouble not the Master.
⁵⁰ But when Jesus heard it, he answered him, saying, Fear not: believe only, and she shall be made whole.
⁵¹ And when he came into the house, he suffered no man to go in, save Peter, and James, and John, and the father and the mother of the maiden.
⁵² And all wept, and bewailed her: but he said, Weep not; she is not dead, but sleepeth.
⁵³ And they laughed him to scorn, knowing that she was dead.
⁵⁴ And he put them all out, and took her by the hand, and called,

saying, Maid, arise.
⁵⁵ And her spirit came again, and she arose straightway: and he commanded to give her meat.
⁵⁶ And her parents were astonished: but he charged them that they should tell no man what was done.

John 4
⁴⁶ So Jesus came again into Cana of Galilee, where he made the water wine. And there was a certain nobleman, whose son was sick at Capernaum.
⁴⁷ When he heard that Jesus was come out of Judaea into Galilee, he went unto him, and besought him that he would come down, and heal his son: for he was at the point of death.
⁴⁸ Then said Jesus unto him, Except ye see signs and wonders, ye will not believe.
⁴⁹ The nobleman saith unto him, Sir, come down ere my child die.
⁵⁰ Jesus saith unto him, Go thy way; thy son liveth. And the man believed the word that Jesus had spoken unto him, and he went his way.
⁵¹ And as he was now going down, his servants met him, and told him, saying, Thy son liveth.
⁵² Then enquired he of them the hour when he began to amend. And they said unto him, Yesterday at the seventh hour the fever left him.
⁵³ So the father knew that it was at the same hour, in the which Jesus said unto him, Thy son liveth: and himself believed, and his whole house.
⁵⁴ This is again the second miracle that Jesus did, when he was come out of Judaea into Galilee.

John 11
¹ Now a certain man was sick, named Lazarus, of Bethany, the town of Mary and her sister Martha.
² (It was that Mary which anointed the Lord with ointment, and wiped his feet with her hair, whose brother Lazarus was sick.)
³ Therefore his sisters sent unto him, saying, Lord, behold, he whom thou lovest is sick.
⁴ When Jesus heard that, he said, This sickness is not unto death, but for the glory of God, that the Son of God might be glorified thereby.
⁵ Now Jesus loved Martha, and her sister, and Lazarus.
⁶ When he had heard therefore that he was sick, he abode two days

still in the same place where he was.
⁷ Then after that saith he to his disciples, Let us go into Judaea again.
⁸ His disciples say unto him, Master, the Jews of late sought to stone thee; and goest thou thither again?
⁹ Jesus answered, Are there not twelve hours in the day? If any man walk in the day, he stumbleth not, because he seeth the light of this world.
¹⁰ But if a man walk in the night, he stumbleth, because there is no light in him.
¹¹ These things said he: and after that he saith unto them, Our friend Lazarus sleepeth; but I go, that I may awake him out of sleep.
¹² Then said his disciples, Lord, if he sleep, he shall do well.
¹³ Howbeit Jesus spake of his death: but they thought that he had spoken of taking of rest in sleep.
¹⁴ Then said Jesus unto them plainly, Lazarus is dead.
¹⁵ And I am glad for your sakes that I was not there, to the intent ye may believe; nevertheless let us go unto him.
¹⁶ Then said Thomas, which is called Didymus, unto his fellowdisciples, Let us also go, that we may die with him.
¹⁷ Then when Jesus came, he found that he had lain in the grave four days already.
¹⁸ Now Bethany was nigh unto Jerusalem, about fifteen furlongs off:
¹⁹ And many of the Jews came to Martha and Mary, to comfort them concerning their brother.
²⁰ Then Martha, as soon as she heard that Jesus was coming, went and met him: but Mary sat still in the house.
²¹ Then said Martha unto Jesus, Lord, if thou hadst been here, my brother had not died.
²² But I know, that even now, whatsoever thou wilt ask of God, God will give it thee.
²³ Jesus saith unto her, Thy brother shall rise again.
²⁴ Martha saith unto him, I know that he shall rise again in the resurrection at the last day.
²⁵ Jesus said unto her, I am the resurrection, and the life: he that believeth in me, though he were dead, yet shall he live:
²⁶ And whosoever liveth and believeth in me shall never die. Believest thou this?
²⁷ She saith unto him, Yea, Lord: I believe that thou art the Christ, the Son of God, which should come into the world.
²⁸ And when she had so said, she went her way, and called Mary her

sister secretly, saying, The Master is come, and calleth for thee.
²⁹ As soon as she heard that, she arose quickly, and came unto him.
³⁰ Now Jesus was not yet come into the town, but was in that place where Martha met him.
³¹ The Jews then which were with her in the house, and comforted her, when they saw Mary, that she rose up hastily and went out, followed her, saying, She goeth unto the grave to weep there.
³² Then when Mary was come where Jesus was, and saw him, she fell down at his feet, saying unto him, Lord, if thou hadst been here, my brother had not died.
³³ When Jesus therefore saw her weeping, and the Jews also weeping which came with her, he groaned in the spirit, and was troubled.
³⁴ And said, Where have ye laid him? They said unto him, Lord, come and see.
³⁵ Jesus wept.
³⁶ Then said the Jews, Behold how he loved him!
³⁷ And some of them said, Could not this man, which opened the eyes of the blind, have caused that even this man should not have died?
³⁸ Jesus therefore again groaning in himself cometh to the grave. It was a cave, and a stone lay upon it.
³⁹ Jesus said, Take ye away the stone. Martha, the sister of him that was dead, saith unto him, Lord, by this time he stinketh: for he hath been dead four days.
⁴⁰ Jesus saith unto her, Said I not unto thee, that, if thou wouldest believe, thou shouldest see the glory of God?
⁴¹ Then they took away the stone from the place where the dead was laid. And Jesus lifted up his eyes, and said, Father, I thank thee that thou hast heard me.
⁴² And I knew that thou hearest me always: but because of the people which stand by I said it, that they may believe that thou hast sent me.
⁴³ And when he thus had spoken, he cried with a loud voice, Lazarus, come forth.
⁴⁴ And he that was dead came forth, bound hand and foot with graveclothes: and his face was bound about with a napkin. Jesus saith unto them, Loose him, and let him go.
⁴⁵ Then many of the Jews which came to Mary, and had seen the things which Jesus did, believed on him.
⁴⁶ But some of them went their ways to the Pharisees, and told them what things Jesus had done.

Acts 9

³⁶ Now there was at Joppa a certain disciple named Tabitha, which by interpretation is called Dorcas: this woman was full of good works and almsdeeds which she did.

³⁷ And it came to pass in those days, that she was sick, and died: whom when they had washed, they laid her in an upper chamber.

³⁸ And forasmuch as Lydda was nigh to Joppa, and the disciples had heard that Peter was there, they sent unto him two men, desiring him that he would not delay to come to them.

³⁹ Then Peter arose and went with them. When he was come, they brought him into the upper chamber: and all the widows stood by him weeping, and shewing the coats and garments which Dorcas made, while she was with them.

⁴⁰ But Peter put them all forth, and kneeled down, and prayed; and turning him to the body said, Tabitha, arise. And she opened her eyes: and when she saw Peter, she sat up.

⁴¹ And he gave her his hand, and lifted her up, and when he had called the saints and widows, presented her alive.

⁴² And it was known throughout all Joppa; and many believed in the Lord.

Acts 20

⁷ And upon the first day of the week, when the disciples came together to break bread, Paul preached unto them, ready to depart on the morrow; and continued his speech until midnight.

⁸ And there were many lights in the upper chamber, where they were gathered together.

⁹ And there sat in a window a certain young man named Eutychus, being fallen into a deep sleep: and as Paul was long preaching, he sunk down with sleep, and fell down from the third loft, and was taken up dead.

¹⁰ And Paul went down, and fell on him, and embracing him said, Trouble not yourselves; for his life is in him.

¹¹ When he therefore was come up again, and had broken bread, and eaten, and talked a long while, even till break of day, so he departed.

¹² And they brought the young man alive, and were not a little comforted.

Lepers Cleansed

Matthew 8
2 And, behold, there came a leper and worshipped him, saying, Lord, if thou wilt, thou canst make me clean.
3 And Jesus put forth his hand, and touched him, saying, I will; be thou clean. And immediately his leprosy was cleansed.
4 And Jesus saith unto him, See thou tell no man; but go thy way, shew thyself to the priest, and offer the gift that Moses commanded, for a testimony unto them.

Mark 1
40 And there came a leper to him, beseeching him, and kneeling down to him, and saying unto him, If thou wilt, thou canst make me clean.
41 And Jesus, moved with compassion, put forth his hand, and touched him, and saith unto him, I will; be thou clean.
42 And as soon as he had spoken, immediately the leprosy departed from him, and he was cleansed.
43 And he straitly charged him, and forthwith sent him away;
44 And saith unto him, See thou say nothing to any man: but go thy way, shew thyself to the priest, and offer for thy cleansing those things which Moses commanded, for a testimony unto them.
45 But he went out, and began to publish it much, and to blaze abroad the matter, insomuch that Jesus could no more openly enter into the city, but was without in desert places: and they came to him from every quarter.

Luke 5
12 And it came to pass, when he was in a certain city, behold a man full of leprosy: who seeing Jesus fell on his face, and besought him, saying, Lord, if thou wilt, thou canst make me clean.
13 And he put forth his hand, and touched him, saying, I will: be thou clean. And immediately the leprosy departed from him.
14 And he charged him to tell no man: but go, and shew thyself to the priest, and offer for thy cleansing, according as Moses commanded, for a testimony unto them.

Luke 17
11 And it came to pass, as he went to Jerusalem, that he passed through the midst of Samaria and Galilee.

¹² And as he entered into a certain village, there met him ten men that were lepers, which stood afar off:
¹³ And they lifted up their voices, and said, Jesus, Master, have mercy on us.
¹⁴ And when he saw them, he said unto them, Go shew yourselves unto the priests. And it came to pass, that, as they went, they were cleansed.
¹⁵ And one of them, when he saw that he was healed, turned back, and with a loud voice glorified God,
¹⁶ And fell down on his face at his feet, giving him thanks: and he was a Samaritan.
¹⁷ And Jesus answering said, Were there not ten cleansed? but where are the nine?
¹⁸ There are not found that returned to give glory to God, save this stranger.
¹⁹ And he said unto him, Arise, go thy way: thy faith hath made thee whole.

Paralyzed People Healed

Matthew 8
⁵ And when Jesus was entered into Capernaum, there came unto him a centurion, beseeching him,
⁶ And saying, Lord, my servant lieth at home sick of the palsy, grievously tormented.
⁷ And Jesus saith unto him, I will come and heal him.
⁸ The centurion answered and said, Lord, I am not worthy that thou shouldest come under my roof: but speak the word only, and my servant shall be healed.
⁹ For I am a man under authority, having soldiers under me: and I say to this man, Go, and he goeth; and to another, Come, and he cometh; and to my servant, Do this, and he doeth it.
¹⁰ When Jesus heard it, he marvelled, and said to them that followed, Verily I say unto you, I have not found so great faith, no, not in Israel.
¹¹ And I say unto you, That many shall come from the east and west, and shall sit down with Abraham, and Isaac, and Jacob, in the kingdom of heaven.
¹² But the children of the kingdom shall be cast out into outer darkness: there shall be weeping and gnashing of teeth.
¹³ And Jesus said unto the centurion, Go thy way; and as thou hast

believed, so be it done unto thee. And his servant was healed in the selfsame hour.

Matthew 9
² And, behold, they brought to him a man sick of the palsy, lying on a bed: and Jesus seeing their faith said unto the sick of the palsy; Son, be of good cheer; thy sins be forgiven thee.
³ And, behold, certain of the scribes said within themselves, This man blasphemeth.
⁴ And Jesus knowing their thoughts said, Wherefore think ye evil in your hearts?
⁵ For whether is easier, to say, Thy sins be forgiven thee; or to say, Arise, and walk?
⁶ But that ye may know that the Son of man hath power on earth to forgive sins, (then saith he to the sick of the palsy,) Arise, take up thy bed, and go unto thine house.
⁷ And he arose, and departed to his house.
⁸ But when the multitudes saw it, they marvelled, and glorified God, which had given such power unto men.

Mark 2
¹ And again he entered into Capernaum after some days; and it was noised that he was in the house.
² And straightway many were gathered together, insomuch that there was no room to receive them, no, not so much as about the door: and he preached the word unto them.
³ And they come unto him, bringing one sick of the palsy, which was borne of four.
⁴ And when they could not come nigh unto him for the press, they uncovered the roof where he was: and when they had broken it up, they let down the bed wherein the sick of the palsy lay.
⁵ When Jesus saw their faith, he said unto the sick of the palsy, Son, thy sins be forgiven thee.
⁶ But there was certain of the scribes sitting there, and reasoning in their hearts,
⁷ Why doth this man thus speak blasphemies? who can forgive sins but God only?
⁸ And immediately when Jesus perceived in his spirit that they so reasoned within themselves, he said unto them, Why reason ye these things in your hearts?

⁹ Whether is it easier to say to the sick of the palsy, Thy sins be forgiven thee; or to say, Arise, and take up thy bed, and walk?
¹⁰ But that ye may know that the Son of man hath power on earth to forgive sins, (he saith to the sick of the palsy,)
¹¹ I say unto thee, Arise, and take up thy bed, and go thy way into thine house.
¹² And immediately he arose, took up the bed, and went forth before them all; insomuch that they were all amazed, and glorified God, saying, We never saw it on this fashion.

Luke 5
¹⁷ And it came to pass on a certain day, as he was teaching, that there were Pharisees and doctors of the law sitting by, which were come out of every town of Galilee, and Judaea, and Jerusalem: and the power of the Lord was present to heal them.
¹⁸ And, behold, men brought in a bed a man which was taken with a palsy: and they sought means to bring him in, and to lay him before him.
¹⁹ And when they could not find by what way they might bring him in because of the multitude, they went upon the housetop, and let him down through the tiling with his couch into the midst before Jesus.
²⁰ And when he saw their faith, he said unto him, Man, thy sins are forgiven thee.
²¹ And the scribes and the Pharisees began to reason, saying, Who is this which speaketh blasphemies? Who can forgive sins, but God alone?
²² But when Jesus perceived their thoughts, he answering said unto them, What reason ye in your hearts?
²³ Whether is easier, to say, Thy sins be forgiven thee; or to say, Rise up and walk?
²⁴ But that ye may know that the Son of man hath power upon earth to forgive sins, (he said unto the sick of the palsy,) I say unto thee, Arise, and take up thy couch, and go into thine house.
²⁵ And immediately he rose up before them, and took up that whereon he lay, and departed to his own house, glorifying God.
²⁶ And they were all amazed, and they glorified God, and were filled with fear, saying, We have seen strange things to day.

Acts 9
³² And it came to pass, as Peter passed throughout all quarters, he

came down also to the saints which dwelt at Lydda.
³³ And there he found a certain man named Aeneas, which had kept his bed eight years, and was sick of the palsy.
³⁴ And Peter said unto him, Aeneas, Jesus Christ maketh thee whole: arise, and make thy bed. And he arose immediately.
³⁵ And all that dwelt at Lydda and Saron saw him, and turned to the Lord.

[See also Matt. 4:24]

People with Fevers Healed

Matthew 8
¹⁴ And when Jesus was come into Peter's house, he saw his wife's mother laid, and sick of a fever.
¹⁵ And he touched her hand, and the fever left her: and she arose, and ministered unto them.

Mark 1
²⁹ And forthwith, when they were come out of the synagogue, they entered into the house of Simon and Andrew, with James and John.
³⁰ But Simon's wife's mother lay sick of a fever, and anon they tell him of her.
³¹ And he came and took her by the hand, and lifted her up; and immediately the fever left her, and she ministered unto them.

Luke 4
³⁸ And he arose out of the synagogue, and entered into Simon's house. And Simon's wife's mother was taken with a great fever; and they besought him for her.
³⁹ And he stood over her, and rebuked the fever; and it left her: and immediately she arose and ministered unto them.

[See also John 4:46-54]

Woman with the Hemorrhage (or "Flow of Blood") Healed

Matthew 9
²⁰ And, behold, a woman, which was diseased with an issue of blood

twelve years, came behind him, and touched the hem of his garment:
²¹ For she said within herself, If I may but touch his garment, I shall be whole.
²² But Jesus turned him about, and when he saw her, he said, Daughter, be of good comfort; thy faith hath made thee whole. And the woman was made whole from that hour.

Mark 5
²⁵ And a certain woman, which had an issue of blood twelve years,
²⁶ And had suffered many things of many physicians, and had spent all that she had, and was nothing bettered, but rather grew worse,
²⁷ When she had heard of Jesus, came in the press behind, and touched his garment.
²⁸ For she said, If I may touch but his clothes, I shall be whole.
²⁹ And straightway the fountain of her blood was dried up; and she felt in her body that she was healed of that plague.
³⁰ And Jesus, immediately knowing in himself that virtue had gone out of him, turned him about in the press, and said, Who touched my clothes?
³¹ And his disciples said unto him, Thou seest the multitude thronging thee, and sayest thou, Who touched me?
³² And he looked round about to see her that had done this thing.
³³ But the woman fearing and trembling, knowing what was done in her, came and fell down before him, and told him all the truth.
³⁴ And he said unto her, Daughter, thy faith hath made thee whole; go in peace, and be whole of thy plague.

Luke 8
⁴² For he had one only daughter, about twelve years of age, and she lay a dying. But as he went the people thronged him.
⁴³ And a woman having an issue of blood twelve years, which had spent all her living upon physicians, neither could be healed of any,
⁴⁴ Came behind him, and touched the border of his garment: and immediately her issue of blood stanched.
⁴⁵ And Jesus said, Who touched me? When all denied, Peter and they that were with him said, Master, the multitude throng thee and press thee, and sayest thou, Who touched me?
⁴⁶ And Jesus said, Somebody hath touched me: for I perceive that virtue is gone out of me.
⁴⁷ And when the woman saw that she was not hid, she came

trembling, and falling down before him, she declared unto him before all the people for what cause she had touched him, and how she was healed immediately.

48 And he said unto her, Daughter, be of good comfort: thy faith hath made thee whole; go in peace.

Blind People Healed

Matthew 9

27 And when Jesus departed thence, two blind men followed him, crying, and saying, Thou son of David, have mercy on us.

28 And when he was come into the house, the blind men came to him: and Jesus saith unto them, Believe ye that I am able to do this? They said unto him, Yea, Lord.

29 Then touched he their eyes, saying, According to your faith be it unto you.

30 And their eyes were opened; and Jesus straitly charged them, saying, See that no man know it.

31 But they, when they were departed, spread abroad his fame in all that country.

Matthew 20

30 And, behold, two blind men sitting by the way side, when they heard that Jesus passed by, cried out, saying, Have mercy on us, O Lord, thou son of David.

31 And the multitude rebuked them, because they should hold their peace: but they cried the more, saying, Have mercy on us, O Lord, thou son of David.

32 And Jesus stood still, and called them, and said, What will ye that I shall do unto you?

33 They say unto him, Lord, that our eyes may be opened.

34 So Jesus had compassion on them, and touched their eyes: and immediately their eyes received sight, and they followed him.

Mark 8

22 And he cometh to Bethsaida; and they bring a blind man unto him, and besought him to touch him.

23 And he took the blind man by the hand, and led him out of the town; and when he had spit on his eyes, and put his hands upon him, he asked him if he saw ought.

24 And he looked up, and said, I see men as trees, walking.
25 After that he put his hands again upon his eyes, and made him look up: and he was restored, and saw every man clearly.
26 And he sent him away to his house, saying, Neither go into the town, nor tell it to any in the town.

Mark 10
46 And they came to Jericho: and as he went out of Jericho with his disciples and a great number of people, blind Bartimaeus, the son of Timaeus, sat by the highway side begging.
47 And when he heard that it was Jesus of Nazareth, he began to cry out, and say, Jesus, thou son of David, have mercy on me.
48 And many charged him that he should hold his peace: but he cried the more a great deal, Thou son of David, have mercy on me.
49 And Jesus stood still, and commanded him to be called. And they call the blind man, saying unto him, Be of good comfort, rise; he calleth thee.
50 And he, casting away his garment, rose, and came to Jesus.
51 And Jesus answered and said unto him, What wilt thou that I should do unto thee? The blind man said unto him, Lord, that I might receive my sight.
52 And Jesus said unto him, Go thy way; thy faith hath made thee whole. And immediately he received his sight, and followed Jesus in the way.

Luke 18
35 And it came to pass, that as he was come nigh unto Jericho, a certain blind man sat by the way side begging:
36 And hearing the multitude pass by, he asked what it meant.
37 And they told him, that Jesus of Nazareth passeth by.
38 And he cried, saying, Jesus, thou son of David, have mercy on me.
39 And they which went before rebuked him, that he should hold his peace: but he cried so much the more, Thou son of David, have mercy on me.
40 And Jesus stood, and commanded him to be brought unto him: and when he was come near, he asked him,
41 Saying, What wilt thou that I shall do unto thee? And he said, Lord, that I may receive my sight.
42 And Jesus said unto him, Receive thy sight: thy faith hath saved thee.

⁴³ And immediately he received his sight, and followed him, glorifying God: and all the people, when they saw it, gave praise unto God.

John 9
¹ And as Jesus passed by, he saw a man which was blind from his birth.
² And his disciples asked him, saying, Master, who did sin, this man, or his parents, that he was born blind?
³ Jesus answered, Neither hath this man sinned, nor his parents: but that the works of God should be made manifest in him.
⁴ I must work the works of him that sent me, while it is day: the night cometh, when no man can work.
⁵ As long as I am in the world, I am the light of the world.
⁶ When he had thus spoken, he spat on the ground, and made clay of the spittle, and he anointed the eyes of the blind man with the clay,
⁷ And said unto him, Go, wash in the pool of Siloam, (which is by interpretation, Sent.) He went his way therefore, and washed, and came seeing.

[Acts 9
⁸ And Saul arose from the earth; and when his eyes were opened, he saw no man: but they led him by the hand, and brought him into Damascus.
⁹ And he was three days without sight, and neither did eat nor drink.
¹⁰ And there was a certain disciple at Damascus, named Ananias; and to him said the Lord in a vision, Ananias. And he said, Behold, I am here, Lord.
¹¹ And the Lord said unto him, Arise, and go into the street which is called Straight, and enquire in the house of Judas for one called Saul, of Tarsus: for, behold, he prayeth,
¹² And hath seen in a vision a man named Ananias coming in, and putting his hand on him, that he might receive his sight.
¹³ Then Ananias answered, Lord, I have heard by many of this man, how much evil he hath done to thy saints at Jerusalem:
¹⁴ And here he hath authority from the chief priests to bind all that call on thy name.
¹⁵ But the Lord said unto him, Go thy way: for he is a chosen vessel unto me, to bear my name before the Gentiles, and kings, and the children of Israel:

¹⁶ For I will shew him how great things he must suffer for my name's sake.
¹⁷ And Ananias went his way, and entered into the house; and putting his hands on him said, Brother Saul, the Lord, even Jesus, that appeared unto thee in the way as thou camest, hath sent me, that thou mightest receive thy sight, and be filled with the Holy Ghost.
¹⁸ And immediately there fell from his eyes as it had been scales: and he received sight forthwith, and arose, and was baptized.
¹⁹ And when he had received meat, he was strengthened. Then was Saul certain days with the disciples which were at Damascus.]

A Man with a Withered Hand Healed

Matthew 12
¹⁰ And, behold, there was a man which had his hand withered. And they asked him, saying, Is it lawful to heal on the sabbath days? that they might accuse him.
¹¹ And he said unto them, What man shall there be among you, that shall have one sheep, and if it fall into a pit on the sabbath day, will he not lay hold on it, and lift it out?
¹² How much then is a man better than a sheep? Wherefore it is lawful to do well on the sabbath days.
¹³ Then saith he to the man, Stretch forth thine hand. And he stretched it forth; and it was restored whole, like as the other.

Mark 3
¹ And he entered again into the synagogue; and there was a man there which had a withered hand.
² And they watched him, whether he would heal him on the sabbath day; that they might accuse him.
³ And he saith unto the man which had the withered hand, Stand forth.
⁴ And he saith unto them, Is it lawful to do good on the sabbath days, or to do evil? to save life, or to kill? But they held their peace.
⁵ And when he had looked round about on them with anger, being grieved for the hardness of their hearts, he saith unto the man, Stretch forth thine hand. And he stretched it out: and his hand was restored whole as the other.

Luke 6

⁶ And it came to pass also on another sabbath, that he entered into the synagogue and taught: and there was a man whose right hand was withered.

⁷ And the scribes and Pharisees watched him, whether he would heal on the sabbath day; that they might find an accusation against him.

⁸ But he knew their thoughts, and said to the man which had the withered hand, Rise up, and stand forth in the midst. And he arose and stood forth.

⁹ Then said Jesus unto them, I will ask you one thing; Is it lawful on the sabbath days to do good, or to do evil? to save life, or to destroy it?

¹⁰ And looking round about upon them all, he said unto the man, Stretch forth thy hand. And he did so: and his hand was restored whole as the other.

¹¹ And they were filled with madness; and communed one with another what they might do to Jesus.

Man with Dropsy (or Edema) Healed

Luke 14

¹ And it came to pass, as he went into the house of one of the chief Pharisees to eat bread on the sabbath day, that they watched him.

² And, behold, there was a certain man before him which had the dropsy.

³ And Jesus answering spake unto the lawyers and Pharisees, saying, Is it lawful to heal on the sabbath day?

⁴ And they held their peace. And he took him, and healed him, and let him go;

⁵ And answered them, saying, Which of you shall have an ass or an ox fallen into a pit, and will not straightway pull him out on the sabbath day?

⁶ And they could not answer him again to these things.

A Man with an Infirmity 38 Years Healed

John 5

¹ After this there was a feast of the Jews; and Jesus went up to Jerusalem.

² Now there is at Jerusalem by the sheep market a pool, which is called in the Hebrew tongue Bethesda, having five porches.

³ In these lay a great multitude of impotent folk, of blind, halt, withered, waiting for the moving of the water.
⁴ For an angel went down at a certain season into the pool, and troubled the water: whosoever then first after the troubling of the water stepped in was made whole of whatsoever disease he had.
⁵ And a certain man was there, which had an infirmity thirty and eight years.
⁶ When Jesus saw him lie, and knew that he had been now a long time in that case, he saith unto him, Wilt thou be made whole?
⁷ The impotent man answered him, Sir, I have no man, when the water is troubled, to put me into the pool: but while I am coming, another steppeth down before me.
⁸ Jesus saith unto him, Rise, take up thy bed, and walk.
⁹ And immediately the man was made whole, and took up his bed, and walked: and on the same day was the sabbath.
¹⁰ The Jews therefore said unto him that was cured, It is the sabbath day: it is not lawful for thee to carry thy bed.
¹¹ He answered them, He that made me whole, the same said unto me, Take up thy bed, and walk.
¹² Then asked they him, What man is that which said unto thee, Take up thy bed, and walk?
¹³ And he that was healed wist not who it was: for Jesus had conveyed himself away, a multitude being in that place.
¹⁴ Afterward Jesus findeth him in the temple, and said unto him, Behold, thou art made whole: sin no more, lest a worse thing come unto thee.
¹⁵ The man departed, and told the Jews that it was Jesus, which had made him whole.

Lame People Healed

Acts 3
¹ Now Peter and John went up together into the temple at the hour of prayer, being the ninth hour.
² And a certain man lame from his mother's womb was carried, whom they laid daily at the gate of the temple which is called Beautiful, to ask alms of them that entered into the temple;
³ Who seeing Peter and John about to go into the temple asked an alms.
⁴ And Peter, fastening his eyes upon him with John, said, Look on us.

⁵ And he gave heed unto them, expecting to receive something of them.
⁶ Then Peter said, Silver and gold have I none; but such as I have give I thee: In the name of Jesus Christ of Nazareth rise up and walk.
⁷ And he took him by the right hand, and lifted him up: and immediately his feet and ankle bones received strength.
⁸ And he leaping up stood, and walked, and entered with them into the temple, walking, and leaping, and praising God.
⁹ And all the people saw him walking and praising God:
¹⁰ And they knew that it was he which sat for alms at the Beautiful gate of the temple: and they were filled with wonder and amazement at that which had happened unto him.
¹¹ And as the lame man which was healed held Peter and John, all the people ran together unto them in the porch that is called Solomon's, greatly wondering.
¹² And when Peter saw it, he answered unto the people, Ye men of Israel, why marvel ye at this? or why look ye so earnestly on us, as though by our own power or holiness we had made this man to walk?
¹³ The God of Abraham, and of Isaac, and of Jacob, the God of our fathers, hath glorified his Son Jesus; whom ye delivered up, and denied him in the presence of Pilate, when he was determined to let him go.
¹⁴ But ye denied the Holy One and the Just, and desired a murderer to be granted unto you;
¹⁵ And killed the Prince of life, whom God hath raised from the dead; whereof we are witnesses.
¹⁶ And his name through faith in his name hath made this man strong, whom ye see and know: yea, the faith which is by him hath given him this perfect soundness in the presence of you all.

Acts 14
⁶ They were ware of it, and fled unto Lystra and Derbe, cities of Lycaonia, and unto the region that lieth round about:
⁷ And there they preached the gospel.
⁸ And there sat a certain man at Lystra, impotent in his feet, being a cripple [or "lame," Strong's # 5560, *cholos*] from his mother's womb, who never had walked:
⁹ The same heard Paul speak: who stedfastly beholding him, and perceiving that he had faith to be healed,

¹⁰ Said with a loud voice, Stand upright on thy feet. And he leaped and walked.

People Who Were Lunatick Were Healed

Matthew 4
²⁴ And his fame went throughout all Syria: and they brought unto him all sick people that were taken with divers diseases and torments, and those which were possessed with devils, and those which were lunatick, and those that had the palsy; and he healed them.

[See also Matt. 17:15]

Several Types of Sickness and Disease Healed in the Same Setting

Matthew 4
²³ And Jesus went about all Galilee, teaching in their synagogues, and preaching the gospel of the kingdom, and healing all manner of sickness and all manner of disease among the people.
²⁴ And his fame went throughout all Syria: and they brought unto him all sick people that were taken with divers diseases and torments, and those which were possessed with devils, and those which were lunatick, and those that had the palsy; and he healed them.

Matthew 8
¹⁶ When the even was come, they brought unto him many that were possessed with devils: and he cast out the spirits with his word, and healed all that were sick:
¹⁷ That it might be fulfilled which was spoken by Esaias the prophet, saying, Himself took our infirmities, and bare our sicknesses.

Matthew 9
³⁵ And Jesus went about all the cities and villages, teaching in their synagogues, and preaching the gospel of the kingdom, and healing every sickness and every disease among the people.

Matthew 14
¹⁴ And Jesus went forth, and saw a great multitude, and was moved with compassion toward them, and he healed their sick.

Matthew 14
34 And when they were gone over, they came into the land of Gennesaret.
35 And when the men of that place had knowledge of him, they sent out into all that country round about, and brought unto him all that were diseased;
36 And besought him that they might only touch the hem of his garment: and as many as touched were made perfectly whole.

Matthew 15
29 And Jesus departed from thence, and came nigh unto the sea of Galilee; and went up into a mountain, and sat down there.
30 And great multitudes came unto him, having with them those that were lame, blind, dumb, maimed, and many others, and cast them down at Jesus' feet; and he healed them:
31 Insomuch that the multitude wondered, when they saw the dumb to speak, the maimed to be whole, the lame to walk, and the blind to see: and they glorified the God of Israel.

Matthew 19
1 And it came to pass, that when Jesus had finished these sayings, he departed from Galilee, and came into the coasts of Judaea beyond Jordan;
2 And great multitudes followed him; and he healed them there.

Matthew 21
14 And the blind and the lame came to him in the temple; and he healed them

Mark 1
32 And at even, when the sun did set, they brought unto him all that were diseased, and them that were possessed with devils.
33 And all the city was gathered together at the door.
34 And he healed many that were sick of divers diseases, and cast out many devils; and suffered not the devils to speak, because they knew him.

Mark 3
7 But Jesus withdrew himself with his disciples to the sea: and a great

multitude from Galilee followed him, and from Judaea,
⁸ And from Jerusalem, and from Idumaea, and from beyond Jordan; and they about Tyre and Sidon, a great multitude, when they had heard what great things he did, came unto him.
⁹ And he spake to his disciples, that a small ship should wait on him because of the multitude, lest they should throng him.
¹⁰ For he had healed many; insomuch that they pressed upon him for to touch him, as many as had plagues.
¹¹ And unclean spirits, when they saw him, fell down before him, and cried, saying, Thou art the Son of God.
¹² And he straitly charged them that they should not make him known.

Mark 6
¹ And he went out from thence, and came into his own country; and his disciples follow him.
² And when the sabbath day was come, he began to teach in the synagogue: and many hearing him were astonished, saying, From whence hath this man these things? and what wisdom is this which is given unto him, that even such mighty works are wrought by his hands?
³ Is not this the carpenter, the son of Mary, the brother of James, and Joses, and of Juda, and Simon? and are not his sisters here with us? And they were offended at him.
⁴ But Jesus, said unto them, A prophet is not without honour, but in his own country, and among his own kin, and in his own house.
⁵ And he could there do no mighty work, save that he laid his hands upon a few sick folk, and healed them.
⁶ And he marvelled because of their unbelief. And he went round about the villages, teaching.

Mark 6
⁵⁴ And when they were come out of the ship, straightway they knew him,
⁵⁵ And ran through that whole region round about, and began to carry about in beds those that were sick, where they heard he was.
⁵⁶ And whithersoever he entered, into villages, or cities, or country, they laid the sick in the streets, and besought him that they might touch if it were but the border of his garment: and as many as touched him were made whole.

Luke 4
⁴⁰ Now when the sun was setting, all they that had any sick with divers diseases brought them unto him; and he laid his hands on every one of them, and healed them.
⁴¹ And devils also came out of many, crying out, and saying, Thou art Christ the Son of God. And he rebuking them suffered them not to speak: for they knew that he was Christ.

Luke 5
¹⁵ But so much the more went there a fame abroad of him: and great multitudes came together to hear, and to be healed by him of their infirmities.

Luke 6
¹² And it came to pass in those days, that he went out into a mountain to pray, and continued all night in prayer to God.
¹³ And when it was day, he called unto him his disciples: and of them he chose twelve, whom also he named apostles;
¹⁷ And he came down with them, and stood in the plain, and the company of his disciples, and a great multitude of people out of all Judaea and Jerusalem, and from the sea coast of Tyre and Sidon, which came to hear him, and to be healed of their diseases;
¹⁸ And they that were vexed with unclean spirits: and they were healed.
¹⁹ And the whole multitude sought to touch him: for there went virtue out of him, and healed them all.

Luke 7
¹⁸ And the disciples of John shewed him of all these things.
¹⁹ And John calling unto him two of his disciples sent them to Jesus, saying, Art thou he that should come? or look we for another?
²⁰ When the men were come unto him, they said, John Baptist hath sent us unto thee, saying, Art thou he that should come? or look we for another?
²¹ And in that same hour he cured many of their infirmities and plagues, and of evil spirits; and unto many that were blind he gave sight.
²² Then Jesus answering said unto them, Go your way, and tell John what things ye have seen and heard; how that the blind see, the lame

walk, the lepers are cleansed, the deaf hear, the dead are raised, to the poor the gospel is preached.
²³ And blessed is he, whosoever shall not be offended in me.

Luke 8
¹ And it came to pass afterward, that he went throughout every city and village, preaching and shewing the glad tidings of the kingdom of God: and the twelve were with him,
² And certain women, which had been healed of evil spirits and infirmities, Mary called Magdalene, out of whom went seven devils,
³ And Joanna the wife of Chuza Herod's steward, and Susanna, and many others, which ministered unto him of their substance.

Luke 9
¹⁰ And the apostles, when they were returned, told him all that they had done. And he took them, and went aside privately into a desert place belonging to the city called Bethsaida.
¹¹ And the people, when they knew it, followed him: and he received them, and spake unto them of the kingdom of God, and healed them that had need of healing.

John 6
² And a great multitude followed him, because they saw his miracles which he did on them that were diseased.

Acts 5
¹² And by the hands of the apostles were many signs and wonders wrought among the people; (and they were all with one accord in Solomon's porch.
¹³ And of the rest durst no man join himself to them: but the people magnified them.
¹⁴ And believers were the more added to the Lord, multitudes both of men and women.)
¹⁵ Insomuch that they brought forth the sick into the streets, and laid them on beds and couches, that at the least the shadow of Peter passing by might overshadow some of them.
¹⁶ There came also a multitude out of the cities round about unto Jerusalem, bringing sick folks, and them which were vexed with unclean spirits: and they were healed every one.

Acts 8
⁵ Then Philip went down to the city of Samaria, and preached Christ unto them.
⁶ And the people with one accord gave heed unto those things which Philip spake, hearing and seeing the miracles which he did.
⁷ For unclean spirits, crying with loud voice, came out of many that were possessed with them: and many taken with palsies, and that were lame, were healed.
⁸ And there was great joy in that city.

Acts 19
¹¹ And God wrought special miracles by the hands of Paul:
¹² So that from his body were brought unto the sick handkerchiefs or aprons, and the diseases departed from them, and the evil spirits went out of them.

Evil Spirits Cast Out

Matthew 4
²³ And Jesus went about all Galilee, teaching in their synagogues, and preaching the gospel of the kingdom, and healing all manner of sickness and all manner of disease among the people.
²⁴ And his fame went throughout all Syria: and they brought unto him all sick people that were taken with divers diseases and torments, and those which were possessed with devils, and those which were lunatick, and those that had the palsy; and he healed them.

Matthew 8
¹⁶ When the even was come, they brought unto him many that were possessed with devils: and he cast out the spirits with his word, and healed all that were sick:
¹⁷ That it might be fulfilled which was spoken by Esaias the prophet, saying, Himself took our infirmities, and bare our sicknesses.

Matthew 8
²⁸ And when he was come to the other side into the country of the Gergesenes, there met him two possessed with devils, coming out of the tombs, exceeding fierce, so that no man might pass by that way.
²⁹ And, behold, they cried out, saying, What have we to do with thee, Jesus, thou Son of God? art thou come hither to torment us before the

time?
³⁰ And there was a good way off from them an herd of many swine feeding.
³¹ So the devils besought him, saying, If thou cast us out, suffer us to go away into the herd of swine.
³² And he said unto them, Go. And when they were come out, they went into the herd of swine: and, behold, the whole herd of swine ran violently down a steep place into the sea, and perished in the waters.
³³ And they that kept them fled, and went their ways into the city, and told every thing, and what was befallen to the possessed of the devils.
³⁴ And, behold, the whole city came out to meet Jesus: and when they saw him, they besought him that he would depart out of their coasts.

Matthew 9
³² As they went out, behold, they brought to him a dumb man possessed with a devil.
³³ And when the devil was cast out, the dumb spake: and the multitudes marvelled, saying, It was never so seen in Israel.
³⁴ But the Pharisees said, He casteth out devils through the prince of the devils.

Matthew 12
²² Then was brought unto him one possessed with a devil, blind, and dumb: and he healed him, insomuch that the blind and dumb both spake and saw.
²³ And all the people were amazed, and said, Is not this the son of David?
²⁴ But when the Pharisees heard it, they said, This fellow doth not cast out devils, but by Beelzebub the prince of the devils.

Matthew 15
²¹ Then Jesus went thence, and departed into the coasts of Tyre and Sidon.
²² And, behold, a woman of Canaan came out of the same coasts, and cried unto him, saying, Have mercy on me, O Lord, thou son of David; my daughter is grievously vexed with a devil.
²³ But he answered her not a word. And his disciples came and besought him, saying, Send her away; for she crieth after us.
²⁴ But he answered and said, I am not sent but unto the lost sheep of the house of Israel.

²⁵ Then came she and worshipped him, saying, Lord, help me.
²⁶ But he answered and said, It is not meet to take the children's bread, and to cast it to dogs.
²⁷ And she said, Truth, Lord: yet the dogs eat of the crumbs which fall from their masters' table.
²⁸ Then Jesus answered and said unto her, O woman, great is thy faith: be it unto thee even as thou wilt. And her daughter was made whole from that very hour.

Matthew 17
¹⁴ And when they were come to the multitude, there came to him a certain man, kneeling down to him, and saying,
¹⁵ Lord, have mercy on my son: for he is lunatick, and sore vexed: for ofttimes he falleth into the fire, and oft into the water.
¹⁶ And I brought him to thy disciples, and they could not cure him.
¹⁷ Then Jesus answered and said, O faithless and perverse generation, how long shall I be with you? how long shall I suffer you? bring him hither to me.
¹⁸ And Jesus rebuked the devil; and he departed out of him: and the child was cured from that very hour.
¹⁹ Then came the disciples to Jesus apart, and said, Why could not we cast him out?
²⁰ And Jesus said unto them, Because of your unbelief: for verily I say unto you, If ye have faith as a grain of mustard seed, ye shall say unto this mountain, Remove hence to yonder place; and it shall remove; and nothing shall be impossible unto you.
²¹ Howbeit this kind goeth not out but by prayer and fasting.

Mark 1
²¹ And they went into Capernaum; and straightway on the sabbath day he entered into the synagogue, and taught.
²² And they were astonished at his doctrine: for he taught them as one that had authority, and not as the scribes.
²³ And there was in their synagogue a man with an unclean spirit; and he cried out,
²⁴ Saying, Let us alone; what have we to do with thee, thou Jesus of Nazareth? art thou come to destroy us? I know thee who thou art, the Holy One of God.
²⁵ And Jesus rebuked him, saying, Hold thy peace, and come out of him.

²⁶ And when the unclean spirit had torn him, and cried with a loud voice, he came out of him.
²⁷ And they were all amazed, insomuch that they questioned among themselves, saying, What thing is this? what new doctrine is this? for with authority commandeth he even the unclean spirits, and they do obey him.
²⁸ And immediately his fame spread abroad throughout all the region round about Galilee.

Mark 1
³² And at even, when the sun did set, they brought unto him all that were diseased, and them that were possessed with devils.
³³ And all the city was gathered together at the door.
³⁴ And he healed many that were sick of divers diseases, and cast out many devils; and suffered not the devils to speak, because they knew him.

Mark 1
³⁹ And he preached in their synagogues throughout all Galilee, and cast out devils.

Mark 3
⁷ But Jesus withdrew himself with his disciples to the sea: and a great multitude from Galilee followed him, and from Judaea,
⁸ And from Jerusalem, and from Idumaea, and from beyond Jordan; and they about Tyre and Sidon, a great multitude, when they had heard what great things he did, came unto him.
⁹ And he spake to his disciples, that a small ship should wait on him because of the multitude, lest they should throng him.
¹⁰ For he had healed many; insomuch that they pressed upon him for to touch him, as many as had plagues.
¹¹ And unclean spirits, when they saw him, fell down before him, and cried, saying, Thou art the Son of God.
¹² And he straitly charged them that they should not make him known.

Mark 5
¹ And they came over unto the other side of the sea, into the country of the Gadarenes.
² And when he was come out of the ship, immediately there met him

out of the tombs a man with an unclean spirit,

³ Who had his dwelling among the tombs; and no man could bind him, no, not with chains:

⁴ Because that he had been often bound with fetters and chains, and the chains had been plucked asunder by him, and the fetters broken in pieces: neither could any man tame him.

⁵ And always, night and day, he was in the mountains, and in the tombs, crying, and cutting himself with stones.

⁶ But when he saw Jesus afar off, he ran and worshipped him,

⁷ And cried with a loud voice, and said, What have I to do with thee, Jesus, thou Son of the most high God? I adjure thee by God, that thou torment me not.

⁸ For he said unto him, Come out of the man, thou unclean spirit.

⁹ And he asked him, What is thy name? And he answered, saying, My name is Legion: for we are many.

¹⁰ And he besought him much that he would not send them away out of the country.

¹¹ Now there was there nigh unto the mountains a great herd of swine feeding.

¹² And all the devils besought him, saying, Send us into the swine, that we may enter into them.

¹³ And forthwith Jesus gave them leave. And the unclean spirits went out, and entered into the swine: and the herd ran violently down a steep place into the sea, (they were about two thousand;) and were choked in the sea.

¹⁴ And they that fed the swine fled, and told it in the city, and in the country. And they went out to see what it was that was done.

¹⁵ And they come to Jesus, and see him that was possessed with the devil, and had the legion, sitting, and clothed, and in his right mind: and they were afraid.

¹⁶ And they that saw it told them how it befell to him that was possessed with the devil, and also concerning the swine.

¹⁷ And they began to pray him to depart out of their coasts.

¹⁸ And when he was come into the ship, he that had been possessed with the devil prayed him that he might be with him.

¹⁹ Howbeit Jesus suffered him not, but saith unto him, Go home to thy friends, and tell them how great things the Lord hath done for thee, and hath had compassion on thee.

²⁰ And he departed, and began to publish in Decapolis how great things Jesus had done for him: and all men did marvel.

Mark 7

²⁴ And from thence he arose, and went into the borders of Tyre and Sidon, and entered into an house, and would have no man know it: but he could not be hid.
²⁵ For a certain woman, whose young daughter had an unclean spirit, heard of him, and came and fell at his feet:
²⁶ The woman was a Greek, a Syrophenician by nation; and she besought him that he would cast forth the devil out of her daughter.
²⁷ But Jesus said unto her, Let the children first be filled: for it is not meet to take the children's bread, and to cast it unto the dogs.
²⁸ And she answered and said unto him, Yes, Lord: yet the dogs under the table eat of the children's crumbs.
²⁹ And he said unto her, For this saying go thy way; the devil is gone out of thy daughter.
³⁰ And when she was come to her house, she found the devil gone out, and her daughter laid upon the bed.

Mark 9

¹⁴ And when he came to his disciples, he saw a great multitude about them, and the scribes questioning with them.
¹⁵ And straightway all the people, when they beheld him, were greatly amazed, and running to him saluted him.
¹⁶ And he asked the scribes, What question ye with them?
¹⁷ And one of the multitude answered and said, Master, I have brought unto thee my son, which hath a dumb spirit;
¹⁸ And wheresoever he taketh him, he teareth him: and he foameth, and gnasheth with his teeth, and pineth away: and I spake to thy disciples that they should cast him out; and they could not.
¹⁹ He answereth him, and saith, O faithless generation, how long shall I be with you? how long shall I suffer you? bring him unto me.
²⁰ And they brought him unto him: and when he saw him, straightway the spirit tare him; and he fell on the ground, and wallowed foaming.
²¹ And he asked his father, How long is it ago since this came unto him? And he said, Of a child.
²² And ofttimes it hath cast him into the fire, and into the waters, to destroy him: but if thou canst do any thing, have compassion on us, and help us.
²³ Jesus said unto him, If thou canst believe, all things are possible to him that believeth.

24 And straightway the father of the child cried out, and said with tears, Lord, I believe; help thou mine unbelief.
25 When Jesus saw that the people came running together, he rebuked the foul spirit, saying unto him, Thou dumb and deaf spirit, I charge thee, come out of him, and enter no more into him.
26 And the spirit cried, and rent him sore, and came out of him: and he was as one dead; insomuch that many said, He is dead.
27 But Jesus took him by the hand, and lifted him up; and he arose.
28 And when he was come into the house, his disciples asked him privately, Why could not we cast him out?
29 And he said unto them, This kind can come forth by nothing, but by prayer and fasting.

Luke 4
31 And came down to Capernaum, a city of Galilee, and taught them on the sabbath days.
32 And they were astonished at his doctrine: for his word was with power.
33 And in the synagogue there was a man, which had a spirit of an unclean devil, and cried out with a loud voice,
34 Saying, Let us alone; what have we to do with thee, thou Jesus of Nazareth? art thou come to destroy us? I know thee who thou art; the Holy One of God.
35 And Jesus rebuked him, saying, Hold thy peace, and come out of him. And when the devil had thrown him in the midst, he came out of him, and hurt him not.
36 And they were all amazed, and spake among themselves, saying, What a word is this! for with authority and power he commandeth the unclean spirits, and they come out.
37 And the fame of him went out into every place of the country round about.

Luke 4
40 Now when the sun was setting, all they that had any sick with divers diseases brought them unto him; and he laid his hands on every one of them, and healed them.
41 And devils also came out of many, crying out, and saying, Thou art Christ the Son of God. And he rebuking them suffered them not to speak: for they knew that he was Christ.

Luke 6
¹² And it came to pass in those days, that he went out into a mountain to pray, and continued all night in prayer to God.
¹³ And when it was day, he called unto him his disciples: and of them he chose twelve, whom also he named apostles;
¹⁷ And he came down with them, and stood in the plain, and the company of his disciples, and a great multitude of people out of all Judaea and Jerusalem, and from the sea coast of Tyre and Sidon, which came to hear him, and to be healed of their diseases;
¹⁸ And they that were vexed with unclean spirits: and they were healed.
¹⁹ And the whole multitude sought to touch him: for there went virtue out of him, and healed them all.

Luke 7
¹⁸ And the disciples of John shewed him of all these things.
¹⁹ And John calling unto him two of his disciples sent them to Jesus, saying, Art thou he that should come? or look we for another?
²⁰ When the men were come unto him, they said, John Baptist hath sent us unto thee, saying, Art thou he that should come? or look we for another?
²¹ And in that same hour he cured many of their infirmities and plagues, and of evil spirits; and unto many that were blind he gave sight.
²² Then Jesus answering said unto them, Go your way, and tell John what things ye have seen and heard; how that the blind see, the lame walk, the lepers are cleansed, the deaf hear, the dead are raised, to the poor the gospel is preached.
²³ And blessed is he, whosoever shall not be offended in me.

Luke 8
¹ And it came to pass afterward, that he went throughout every city and village, preaching and shewing the glad tidings of the kingdom of God: and the twelve were with him,
² And certain women, which had been healed of evil spirits and infirmities, Mary called Magdalene, out of whom went seven devils,
³ And Joanna the wife of Chuza Herod's steward, and Susanna, and many others, which ministered unto him of their substance.

Luke 8

26 And they arrived at the country of the Gadarenes, which is over against Galilee.

27 And when he went forth to land, there met him out of the city a certain man, which had devils long time, and ware no clothes, neither abode in any house, but in the tombs.

28 When he saw Jesus, he cried out, and fell down before him, and with a loud voice said, What have I to do with thee, Jesus, thou Son of God most high? I beseech thee, torment me not.

29 (For he had commanded the unclean spirit to come out of the man. For oftentimes it had caught him: and he was kept bound with chains and in fetters; and he brake the bands, and was driven of the devil into the wilderness.)

30 And Jesus asked him, saying, What is thy name? And he said, Legion: because many devils were entered into him.

31 And they besought him that he would not command them to go out into the deep.

32 And there was there an herd of many swine feeding on the mountain: and they besought him that he would suffer them to enter into them. And he suffered them.

33 Then went the devils out of the man, and entered into the swine: and the herd ran violently down a steep place into the lake, and were choked.

34 When they that fed them saw what was done, they fled, and went and told it in the city and in the country.

35 Then they went out to see what was done; and came to Jesus, and found the man, out of whom the devils were departed, sitting at the feet of Jesus, clothed, and in his right mind: and they were afraid.

36 They also which saw it told them by what means he that was possessed of the devils was healed.

37 Then the whole multitude of the country of the Gadarenes round about besought him to depart from them; for they were taken with great fear: and he went up into the ship, and returned back again.

38 Now the man out of whom the devils were departed besought him that he might be with him: but Jesus sent him away, saying,

39 Return to thine own house, and shew how great things God hath done unto thee. And he went his way, and published throughout the whole city how great things Jesus had done unto him.

Luke 9
^{37} And it came to pass, that on the next day, when they were come down from the hill, much people met him.
^{38} And, behold, a man of the company cried out, saying, Master, I beseech thee, look upon my son: for he is mine only child.
^{39} And, lo, a spirit taketh him, and he suddenly crieth out; and it teareth him that he foameth again, and bruising him hardly departeth from him.
^{40} And I besought thy disciples to cast him out; and they could not.
^{41} And Jesus answering said, O faithless and perverse generation, how long shall I be with you, and suffer you? Bring thy son hither.
^{42} And as he was yet a coming, the devil threw him down, and tare him. And Jesus rebuked the unclean spirit, and healed the child, and delivered him again to his father.
^{43} And they were all amazed at the mighty power of God. But while they wondered every one at all things which Jesus did, he said unto his disciples,

Luke 11
^{14} And he was casting out a devil, and it was dumb. And it came to pass, when the devil was gone out, the dumb spake; and the people wondered.

Luke 13
^{10} And he was teaching in one of the synagogues on the sabbath.
^{11} And, behold, there was a woman which had a spirit of infirmity eighteen years, and was bowed together, and could in no wise lift up herself.
^{12} And when Jesus saw her, he called her to him, and said unto her, Woman, thou art loosed from thine infirmity.
^{13} And he laid his hands on her: and immediately she was made straight, and glorified God.
^{14} And the ruler of the synagogue answered with indignation, because that Jesus had healed on the sabbath day, and said unto the people, There are six days in which men ought to work: in them therefore come and be healed, and not on the sabbath day.
^{15} The Lord then answered him, and said, Thou hypocrite, doth not each one of you on the sabbath loose his ox or his ass from the stall, and lead him away to watering?
^{16} And ought not this woman, being a daughter of Abraham, whom

Satan hath bound, lo, these eighteen years, be loosed from this bond on the sabbath day?

¹⁷ And when he had said these things, all his adversaries were ashamed: and all the people rejoiced for all the glorious things that were done by him.

Acts 8

⁵ Then Philip went down to the city of Samaria, and preached Christ unto them.

⁶ And the people with one accord gave heed unto those things which Philip spake, hearing and seeing the miracles which he did.

⁷ For unclean spirits, crying with loud voice, came out of many that were possessed with them: and many taken with palsies, and that were lame, were healed.

⁸ And there was great joy in that city.

Acts 16

¹⁶ And it came to pass, as we went to prayer, a certain damsel possessed with a spirit of divination met us, which brought her masters much gain by soothsaying:

¹⁷ The same followed Paul and us, and cried, saying, These men are the servants of the most high God, which shew unto us the way of salvation.

¹⁸ And this did she many days. But Paul, being grieved, turned and said to the spirit, I command thee in the name of Jesus Christ to come out of her. And he came out the same hour.

Acts 19

¹¹ And God wrought special miracles by the hands of Paul:

¹² So that from his body were brought unto the sick handkerchiefs or aprons, and the diseases departed from them, and the evil spirits went out of them.

Index

1 Corinthians 13, 8, 15, 53, 74, 75, 76, 77, 80, 85, 91, 103
12 Steps, 19, 80

A

A.A. pioneers, 3, 54, 67, 74, 76, 77
Absolute Essentials, vii, 15, 90
Abstain, 49
Abstinence, ix, 26, 27, 28, 29, 85, 89, 94, 107, 113, 114
Addict, x
Admission, 93
Akron, vii, x, xi, 4, 5, 6, 7, 8, 9, 10, 11, 12, 13, 15, 16, 17, 18, 24, 29, 32, 33, 44, 45, 46, 48, 55, 59, 60, 65, 69, 72, 77, 79, 80, 81, 82, 83, 84, 85, 86, 88, 89, 91, 92, 93, 94, 97, 99, 102, 104, 108, 112, 156, 158
Al-Anon, 9, 12, 82
Anne Smith, 2, 7, 9, 10, 11, 16, 19, 20, 25, 34, 37, 42, 57, 60, 64, 66, 68, 80, 90, 91, 93, 95, 99, 101, 156, 158
Anonymity, 62
Avoidance, 38, 61

B

Believers, 3, 36, 48

Bible, x, xi, 1, 2, 4, 5, 6, 7, 8, 9, 10, 12, 13, 15, 16, 17, 18, 19, 20, 22, 23, 24, 27, 31, 34, 35, 37, 38, 39, 43, 44, 48, 49, 53, 54, 55, 56, 62, 67, 71, 73, 74, 75, 76, 77, 80, 85, 86, 88, 90, 91, 92, 96, 97, 98, 99, 102, 103, 107, 108, 111, 112, 114, 156, 157, 158
Biblical healings, 1
Biblical roots, 3, 24, 98
Big Book, 2, 8, 15, 17, 18, 19, 20, 23, 24, 25, 30, 31, 32, 33, 34, 35, 37, 38, 39, 40, 41, 42, 43, 44, 45, 48, 54, 55, 56, 57, 60, 63, 64, 65, 66, 68, 69, 70, 72, 76, 77, 79, 80, 81, 82, 83, 86, 87, 88, 89, 91, 92, 96, 97, 98, 99, 102, 156, 158
Bill Dotson, 2, 6, 98
Bill Wilson, 2, 4, 5, 6, 7, 8, 10, 16, 17, 19, 23, 30, 34, 44, 53, 54, 55, 63, 67, 70, 71, 72, 73, 75, 77, 79, 80, 81, 83, 86, 87, 88, 89, 90, 94, 98, 99, 100, 108
Book of James, 8, 15, 16, 17, 18, 19, 20, 23, 24, 26, 29, 33, 34, 40, 42, 44, 45, 48, 49, 53, 57, 78, 80, 85, 91, 103

C

Calvary Rescue Mission, 4, 10, 92
Charity, 74, 75, 76, 103

Christ, 156
Christian, 157
Christian books, 6
Christian Endeavor, 7, 13, 69, 85, 89, 107, 114
Christian fellowship, 3, 50
Church, xi, 1, 6, 8, 9, 10, 11, 22, 45, 47, 85, 90, 108, 111, 112, 157
Clarace Williams, 8
Clarence H. Snyder, 10
Companionship, 41, 103
Compassion, xi, 58, 60, 117, 122, 128, 135, 144, 145
Conference Approved, 13, 17
Confess your faults, 20, 44
Confession, 8, 9, 13, 83, 85, 88, 95
Continuance, 88, 95, 96
Conversion, 2, 13, 85, 86, 87, 88, 92, 94, 95, 99, 158
Conviction, 8, 9, 88, 95
Counseling, 9, 86
Courtesy, 76
Creator, ix, x, 3, 4, 7, 8, 10, 26, 29, 31, 56, 67, 68, 70, 74, 80, 84, 85, 90, 93, 96, 98, 107, 108, 110, 112
Cures, 1, 2

D

Deliverance, 50
Detoxification, ix
Devotionals, 6, 7, 8, 10, 55, 67, 80
Dishonesty, 39, 84, 94, 96
Dr. Bob, 2, 1, 2, 4, 5, 6, 7, 8, 9, 10, 11, 12, 13, 15, 16, 18, 19, 20, 23, 26, 27, 28, 34, 37, 39, 46, 47, 53, 54, 55, 56, 57, 58, 59, 60, 65, 66, 68, 69, 70, 72, 73, 75, 76, 77, 78, 80, 82, 85, 89, 90, 91, 92, 93, 94, 98, 99, 101, 102, 108, 114, 156, 158
Dr. Carl Gustav Jung, 86, 92

E

Early A.A., xi, 2, 87, 90, 92, 156, 158
Early AAs, 2, 156, 158
Ed Webster, 101
Envy, 38
Essentials, 70

F

Faith, 3, 16, 17, 19, 23, 32, 33, 34, 46, 99, 156
Family, x, 7, 8, 9, 10, 11, 13, 29, 75, 111, 112
Family Groups, 12
Father Ed Dowling, 100
Father Ralph Pfau, 100
Fellowship, 156
Firmness, 112
Forgiveness, 43, 44, 63, 64
Four Absolutes, 9, 80, 94, 99
Frank Amos, 4, 5, 6, 80, 90, 97, 102
Fundamentals, 70

G

Generosity, 76
God, ix, x, xi, 1, 2, 3, 5, 7, 8, 9, 10, 13, 15, 20, 21, 22, 24, 25,

26, 27, 29, 30, 31, 32, 33, 35, 36, 38, 39, 40, 41, 42, 43, 44, 45, 47, 48, 49, 50, 51, 52, 53, 56, 57, 58, 59, 60, 61, 62, 63, 64, 65, 67, 68, 70, 71, 72, 73, 74, 76, 77, 78, 80, 81, 82, 83, 84, 88, 89, 91, 92, 93, 94, 95, 96, 97, 98, 100, 102, 103, 104, 105, 107, 108, 110, 111, 112, 113, 114, 117, 118, 123, 124, 125, 130, 134, 136, 137, 138, 139, 140, 142, 143, 144, 146, 147, 148, 149, 150, 156, 158

God's commandments, 21, 36, 52, 107, 108
God's way, 49, 111
God's will, 32, 50, 72, 84, 88, 94
God's Word, ix, x, 27, 39, 113
God-centeredness, 62
God-sufficiency, 62
Good Book, vii, x, 7, 15, 16, 18, 19, 49, 50, 53, 55, 65, 66, 87, 90, 92, 114, 156, 157, 158, 159
Good Temper, 76
Growth in fellowship, 88
Grudges, 42
Guidance, 7, 8, 16, 17, 25, 44, 48, 49, 83, 85, 90, 91, 97, 103, 107

H

Healing, ix, 1, 13, 47, 115
Helping Others, 35
Henrietta Seiberling, 7, 8, 9, 11, 16, 59, 63, 156, 158

Higher Power, 2, 12, 13, 76, 92
Holy Spirit, 1, 84, 98
Honesty, 9
Hospitalization, xi, 80, 89, 90, 99, 103
Humility, 40, 50, 59, 76

I

Inventory, 7, 9, 94

J

Jealousy, 38, 39, 78
Jerry G. Dunn, 27, 110, 111
John D. Rockefeller, Jr., 5, 90
Joy, 30, 64, 113, 140, 150

K

Kindness, 76
Kingdom of Heaven, 57, 58, 59, 70, 123
Knowledge, ix, 12, 26, 70, 94, 100, 136

L

Lois Wilson, 4, 11, 81, 95, 98
Long-Suffering, 112
Lord's Prayer, 18, 20, 27, 54, 72, 98, 103
Love, xi, 9, 33, 34, 60, 61, 69, 74, 75, 76, 77, 103, 108

M

Medically Incurable, x, xi, 4
Meditate, 103
Meetings, ix, x, 2, 4, 7, 8, 10, 11, 13, 15, 16, 20, 26, 48, 50, 53, 54, 55, 56, 64, 85, 90, 98, 104, 107, 110

N

New Testament, 1, 38, 47, 56, 57, 63, 77, 115, 157
Newcomers, ix, x, xi, 8, 9, 10, 11, 48, 80, 90, 110, 114

O

Obedience, 52, 108
Old School A.A., xi
Old Testament, 1, 60, 73, 77
Oswald Chambers, 10, 54, 56, 67, 91
Oxford Group, 2, 4, 7, 8, 9, 10, 11, 16, 20, 23, 25, 34, 42, 43, 44, 45, 54, 55, 56, 60, 62, 64, 71, 72, 79, 80, 81, 82, 83, 87, 88, 89, 91, 92, 93, 94, 95, 96, 97, 98, 99, 100, 101, 107, 114, 156, 158

P

Patience, 21, 24, 42, 59, 76
Peace, 30, 36, 39, 59, 61, 95, 97, 127, 128, 129, 131, 132, 142, 146
Peacemakers, 58, 59
Pioneers, 2, 3
Power of God, 89, 92, 156
Praise, 46, 130
Prayer, 5, 7, 8, 9, 10, 12, 15, 16, 18, 22, 23, 28, 32, 39, 43, 45, 46, 47, 50, 52, 54, 56, 67, 73, 80, 82, 86, 88, 90, 91, 93, 94, 96, 97, 98, 102, 103, 107, 111, 112, 114, 133, 138, 142, 146, 147, 150
Principles, 3, 4, 8, 9, 15, 23, 24, 33, 37, 44, 48, 55, 59, 60, 69, 78, 80, 81, 82, 85, 89, 91, 98, 100, 102, 114
Purity, 9

Q

Quiet Time, 5, 7, 10, 90, 97

R

Real Surrenders, 9
Recovery, x, xi, 2, 3, 4, 6, 10, 13, 29, 48, 59, 66, 78, 80, 83, 89, 98, 100, 101, 156, 157
Religion, xi, 47, 67, 87, 91, 103
Religious Literature, 5, 13, 85, 97
Religious Service, 5
Rescue Missions, 9
Resentments, 61
Resist the devil, 40, 50, 51
Responsibility, 21, 81
Restitution, 8, 9, 83, 88, 96
Richard Peabody, 2, 89, 98
Richmond Walker, 100

Righteousness, 31, 39, 52, 57, 58, 59, 65, 72

S

Salvation, ix, x, 51, 85, 86, 92, 97, 107, 111, 150
Sam Shoemaker, 2, 8, 20, 23, 32, 41, 43, 67, 71, 86, 87, 89, 93, 98, 156, 158
Self-Centeredness, 39, 49, 62, 84, 94
Self-government, 11
Self-Leadership, 11
Serenity Prayer, 20
Sermon on the Mount, 8, 10, 15, 16, 18, 19, 23, 37, 42, 44, 53, 54, 55, 56, 57, 63, 65, 68, 70, 74, 80, 85, 91, 95, 96, 103
Sickness, 49, 118, 135, 140
Sincerity, 76
Sister Ignatia, 99
Sobriety, 4, 11, 16, 29, 54, 77, 79, 82, 100
Spirit, x, 52, 64, 65, 84, 95, 111
Spirit of God, x
Spiritual Growth, 2, 6, 55, 91, 92, 156, 158
Strength, 18, 25, 26, 48, 52, 70, 77, 85, 90, 110, 134
Success Rate, x, xi, 4, 99
Suffering, xi, 36, 59, 85, 87, 93
Sunday School, 156
Support, 3, 7, 11, 12, 13, 86, 97, 101, 107, 108, 113, 114
Surrender, 5, 7, 9, 10, 44, 46, 56, 60, 67, 82, 84, 88, 94, 96

T

T. Henry Williams, 7, 8, 9, 46
Temptation, 21, 24, 25, 26, 27, 28, 29, 30, 31, 33, 41, 42, 49, 50, 52, 56, 85, 90, 113, 114
The Beatitudes, 57
The Runner's Bible, 10, 55, 91
The Salvation Army, 85, 107
Towns Hospital, 4, 10, 16, 87, 92
Treatment Programs, xi
Twelve Step Fellowship, 1, 5, ix
Twelve Steps, 2, 6, 3, 15, 18, 41, 53, 56, 69, 76, 81, 83, 88, 89, 90, 91, 92, 97, 99, 101, 102, 104
Twelve Traditions, 101

U

Unselfishness, 9, 76

V

Victory, 114

W

Wholeness, ix, 114
William Duncan Silkworth, 93, 108
Willpower, 5, 28, 29, 30
Wisdom, 21, 22, 24, 25, 26, 38, 49, 137

Wives and Families, 11
Word of God, 43
Wrongdoing, 42, 61, 78

Y

Yahweh, 31, 56, 60, 67, 70

About the Author

Dick B. writes books on the spiritual roots of Alcoholics Anonymous. They show how the basic and highly successful biblical ideas used by early AAs can be valuable tools for success in today's A.A. His research can also help the religious and recovery communities work more effectively with alcoholics, addicts, and others involved in Twelve Step programs.

      The author is an active, recovered member of A.A.; a retired attorney; and a Bible student. He has sponsored more than one hundred men in their recovery from alcoholism. Consistent with A.A.'s traditions of anonymity, he uses the pseudonym "Dick B."

      He has had twenty-eight titles published including: *Dr. Bob and His Library*; *Anne Smith's Journal, 1933-1939*; *The Oxford Group & Alcoholics Anonymous*; *The Akron Genesis of Alcoholics Anonymous*; *The Books Early AAs Read for Spiritual Growth*; *New Light on Alcoholism: God, Sam Shoemaker, and A.A.*; *Courage to Change* (with Bill Pittman); *Cured: Proven Help for Alcoholics and Addicts; The Good Book and The Big Book: A.A.'s Roots in the Bible*; *That Amazing Grace: The Role of Clarence and Grace S. in Alcoholics Anonymous*; *Good Morning!: Quiet Time, Morning Watch, Meditation, and Early A.A.*; *Turning Point: A History of Early A.A.'s Spiritual Roots and Successes, Hope!: The Story of Geraldine D., Alina Lodge & Recovery; Utilizing Early A.A.'s Spiritual Roots for Recovery Today; The Golden Text of A.A.; By the Power of God; God and Alcoholism; Making Known the Biblical History of A.A.; Why Early A.A. Succeeded*; *Comments of Dick B. at The First Nationwide A.A. History Conference; Henrietta Seiberling: Ohio's Lady with a Cause;* and *The James Club*. The books have been the subject of newspaper articles and reviews in *Library Journal*, *Bookstore Journal*, *The Living Church*, *Faith at Work*, *Sober Times*, *Episcopal Life*, *Recovery News*, *Ohioana Quarterly*, *The PHOENIX*, and *The Saint Louis University Theology Digest*. They are listed in the biographies of major addiction center, religion, and religious history sites. He has published over 150 articles on his subject, most posted on the internet.

      Dick is the father of two sons (Ken and Don) and has two granddaughters. As a young man, he did a stint as a newspaper reporter. He attended the University of California, Berkeley, where he received his A.A. degree with Honorable Mention, majored in economics, and was elected to Phi Beta Kappa in his Junior year. In the United States Army, he was an Information-Education Specialist. He received his A.B. and J.D. degrees from Stanford University, and was Case Editor of the Stanford Law Review. Dick became interested in Bible study in his childhood Sunday School and was much inspired by his mother's almost daily study of Scripture. He joined, and was president of, a Community Church affiliated with the United Church of Christ. By 1972, he was studying the origins of the Bible and began traveling abroad in pursuit of that subject. In 1979, he became much involved in a Biblical research, teaching, and fellowship ministry. In his community life, he was president of a merchants' council, Chamber of Commerce, church retirement center, and homeowners' association. He served on a public district board and has held offices in a service club.

In 1986, he was felled by alcoholism, gave up his law practice, and began recovery as a member of the Fellowship of Alcoholics Anonymous. In 1990, his interest in A.A.'s Biblical/Christian roots was sparked by his attendance at A.A.'s International Convention in Seattle. He has traveled widely; researched at archives, and at public and seminary libraries; interviewed scholars, historians, clergy, A.A. "old-timers" and survivors; and participated in programs and conferences on A.A.'s roots.

The author is the owner of Good Book Publishing Company and has several works in progress. Much of his research and writing is done in collaboration with his older son, Ken, an ordained minister, who holds B.A., B.Th., and M.A. degrees. Ken has been a lecturer in New Testament Greek at a Bible college and a lecturer in Fundamentals of Oral Communication at San Francisco State University. Ken is a computer specialist and director of marketing and research in Hawaii ethanol projects.

Dick is a member of the American Historical Association, Research Society on Alcoholism, Alcohol and Drugs History Society, Organization of American Historians, The Association for Medical Education and Research in Substance Abuse, Coalition of Prison Evangelists, Christian Association for Psychological Studies, and International Substance Abuse and Addictions Coalition. He is available for conferences, panels, seminars, and interviews.

Good Book Publishing Company Order Form

(Use this form to order Dick B.'s titles on early A.A.'s roots and successes)

Qty.	Titles by Dick B.	Price	
____	*A New Way In*	$19.95 ea.	$ _____
____	*A New Way Out*	$19.95 ea.	$ _____
____	*Anne Smith's Journal, 1933-1939*	$22.95 ea.	$ _____
____	*By the Power of God: A Guide to Early A.A. Groups and Forming Similar Groups Today*	$23.95 ea.	$ _____
____	*Cured! Proven Help for Alcoholics and Addicts*	$23.95 ea.	$ _____
____	*Dr. Bob and His Library*	$22.95 ea.	$ _____
____	*Dr. Bob of Alcoholics Anonymous*	$24.95 ea.	$ _____
____	*God and Alcoholism*	$21.95 ea.	$ _____
____	*Good Morning! Quiet Time, Morning Watch, Meditation, and Early A.A.*	$22.95 ea.	$ ✓
____	*Henrietta B. Seiberling*	$20.95 ea.	$ _____
____	*Introduction to the Sources and Founding of A.A.*	$22.95 ea.	$ _____
____	*Making Known the Biblical History and Roots of Alcoholics Anonymous*	$24.95 ea.	$ _____
____	*New Light on Alcoholism: God, Sam Shoemaker, and A.A.*	$24.95 ea.	$ _____
____	*Real Twelve Step Fellowship History*	$23.95 ea.	$ _____
____	*That Amazing Grace: The Role of Clarence and Grace S. in Alcoholics Anonymous*	$22.95 ea.	$ _____
____	*The Akron Genesis of Alcoholics Anonymous*	$23.95 ea.	$ _____
____	*The Books Early AAs Read for Spiritual Growth*	$21.95 ea.	$ _____
____	*The Conversion of Bill W.*	$23.95 ea.	$ _____
____	*The First Nationwide A.A. History Conference*	$22.95 ea.	$ _____
____	*The Golden Text of A.A.*	$20.95 ea.	$ _____
____	*The Good Book and the Big Book: A.A.'s Roots in the Bible*	$23.95 ea.	$ _____
____	*The Good Book-Big Book Guidebook*	$22.95 ea.	$ ✓
____	*The James Club and the Original A.A. Program's Absolute Essentials*	$23.95 ea.	$ _____
____	*The Oxford Group and Alcoholics Anonymous*	$23.95 ea.	$ _____
____	*Turning Point: A History of Early A.A.'s Spiritual Roots and Successes*	$29.95 ea.	$ _____
____	*Twelve Steps for You*	$21.95 ea.	$ _____
____	*Utilizing Early A.A.'s Spiritual Roots for Recovery Today*	$20.95 ea.	$ _____
____	*When Early AAs Were Cured and Why*	$23.95 ea.	$ _____
____	*Why Early A.A. Succeeded*	$23.95 ea.	$ _____

(Order Form continued on the next page)

Good Book Publishing Company Order Form
(continued from the previous page)

Order Subtotal: $ _____

Shipping and Handling (S&H) **: $ _____

(** For Shipping and Handling, please add 10% of the Order Subtotal for U.S. orders or 15% of the Order Subtotal for international orders. The minimum U.S. S&H is $5.60. The minimum S&H for Canada and Mexico is US$ 9.95. The minimum S&H for other countries is US$ 11.95.)

Order Total: $ _____

Credit card: VISA   MasterCard   American Express   Discover   (circle one)

Account number: _____ Exp.: _____

Name: _____ (as it is on your credit card, if using one)

(Company: _____)

Address Line 1: _____

Address Line 2: _____

City: _____ State/Prov.: _____

Zip/Postal Code: _____ Country: _____

Signature: _____ Telephone: _____

Email: _____

No returns accepted. Please mail this Order Form, along with your check or money order (if sending one), to: Dick B., c/o Good Book Publishing Company, PO Box 837, Kihei, HI 96753-0837. Please make your check or money order (if sending one) payable to "Dick B." in U.S. dollars drawn on a U.S. bank. If you have any questions, please phone: 1-808-874-4876 or send an email message to: dickb@dickb.com. Dick B.'s web site: www.DickB.com.

If you would like to purchase Dick B.'s entire 29-volume reference set on early A.A.'s roots and successes (and how those successes may be replicated today) at a substantial discount, please send Dick B. an email message or give him a call.

Paradise Research Publications, Inc.
PO Box 837
Kihei, HI 96753-0837
(808) 874-4876
Email: dickb@dickb.com
URL: http://www.dickb.com/index.shtml
http://www.dickb-blog.com

Made in the USA
Lexington, KY
08 February 2013